It's The *Brain*, Stupid!
A pro-choice defense.
By Eric J. Hildeman

Table of Contents:

Preamble: Oh, The Lengths To Which They'll Go!

In 1962 Gianna Beretta Molla, a mother of three, and pregnant with her fourth, discovered she had a potentially lethal uterine tumor. She faced a horrible predicament which no potential mother should ever have to face: An abortion would kill the fetus she was carrying, while letting it grow to term would likely kill her. She weighed the options and made her choice, telling the doctors not to save her life if it meant terminating the pregnancy. She died a week after giving birth, leaving her husband a widower and her four children motherless. But her sacrifice saved her unborn baby.

On May 16, 2004, Pope John Paul II Canonized her as a Saint, prioritizing her ahead of Mother Teresa for the title.

When it comes to abortion, Christians aren't kidding!

This illustrates fully just how vigorously the religious right stands opposed to abortion. Believers go quite out of their way to defend, "the rights of the preborn," with a passion that goes beyond even that of spreading the Gospel, or (oddly enough) feeding post-natal infants who are starving. Women's advocacy groups, on the other hand, go out of their way to defend the right of a woman to be able to choose her own fate, trying desperately to retain the few, hard-fought gains which have been made for women's rights at a time when even a woman's right to vote is less than a century old. At heart are the two dearest values held by American culture. On the one side, the right to live. On the other side, the right to live free. The fervor over this one issue is enough to ignite the deepest passions in people (thus guaranteeing this book a potential bestseller status). No other issue pisses people off quite as much. No other issue drives people *away* from Christianity quite so effectively, not even evolution in public schools.

Could it actually be that Christians have taken the *wrong* side? Indeed, they have. But not for the reasons you might think.

But first, let's get one thing straight: "Saint Gianna," did a courageous thing. She exercised her right to choose, and she chose the life of her unborn child. She risked her life to save her daughter. Any mother might do the same. But she died as a result, an overall negative – especially for her children. She is quite rightly hailed as a heroic figure. But should the law *require* someone to perform such an act of heroism, saving her children's lives at the expense of their well-being?

If we truly value "right to life," then the answer must be no. This book will explore why.

It will also target the Christian viewpoint of the argument. Although it is acknowledged that there are some non-Christians who stand opposed to abortion, the demographic in America is such that nearly all opposition to abortion comes via Christian leadership. (Though certainly there may be some Judaism or Islam involved as well.) It should be understood that this broad-brush approach is done for the sake of brevity, not because of any assumption that Christians are synonymous with pro-lifers, nor out of any desire to stereotype or marginalize them.

What clearly makes abortion such a contentious issue are the consequences. They are so severely life-changing (some would argue life-ruining) that people want—no, *need*—a clear, unambiguous answer. No matter which side one takes, pro-life or pro-choice, the consequence of dealing with an unplanned, unintended, or unwanted pregnancy is the same – a ruined life. Either it's the ruined life of the teenage mother, or the ruined life of her growing fetus. With consequences so dire, it's no wonder an absolute solution is demanded. There may be just such a clear solution, but ironically, it does not lie in the positions that activists have entrenched themselves in on either side.

Nor does the solution lie within Christian scripture. Perhaps the oddest thing about the abortion debate is that Christians are the driving force behind the pro-life side, despite the Bible clearly having nothing to say in favor of abortion. Abortion didn't exist at the time the Bible was written – the technology for it hadn't been invented yet.[1] There is an element to this book's premise that is Bible-based, and it is truly surprising. For now, we must recognize that it is the *clergy*, not scripture nor the Almighty, who have

---

[1] There were some methods used prior to the era of modern surgery, such as the use of crocodile dung by the ancient Egyptians, or the Romans using silphium. Other methods involved fasting or bloodletting. But these methods were rare, often ineffective, and seldom heard of, especially by men. Only modern abortion techniques made the practice common and safe.

insisted that conception is the point at which an individual's legal rights begin. God, it seems, has decided to remain mute on this particular issue, at least Biblically.

In fact, one of the strangest aspects to the lack of scriptural authority is that no religious leaders have stepped forward claiming "visions" or "divine revelations" as to the point of onset of a living being. (Or, if "visions" are declared, they are so backwater as to not be headline news, as would be the case if a major religious leader such as Pat Robertson or Rick Warren were to claim a revelation from God.) Only modern science is cited in evidence for the pro-life position. This "science-only" approach is a humorously odd twist of fate indeed, given Christianity's remarkably poor track-record of cooperation with science in matters such as evolution, global warming or the heliocentric solar system. But this insistence upon science, while seemingly effective for short-term political gains in recent years, will prove to be the undoing of the anti-abortion movement, as we'll see in a moment.

It's been said before, and it bears repeating here: We are *all* pro-life and pro-choice. It's whether or not one is for or against abortion which is at issue. With that in mind, we can begin to locate common ground. Oh, to be sure, there are a few activists on the pro-choice side who insist that any abortive procedure, even the ones immediately prior to birth, should be legal for contraceptive purposes. There are also a considerable number of activists of the opposite extreme who insist that any form of contraception should be illegal. But are these the only two places where we can reasonably draw the line? Come to think of it, are *either* of these two options reasonable?

As we are about to see, the answer is no – to both questions.

Introduction: Birth vs. Conception

Let's begin with a concession to the pro-life side of the argument. The only real difference between a fetus just before birth and a baby just after birth is that the latter breathes air, and the former breathes amniotic fluid. (As well as taking in sustenance by drinking milk as opposed to having an umbilical cord.) Thus, the argument that birth is not a reasonable place to draw the line is not only sound, it's a scientific fact. We must always bow to the scientific evidence regardless of our political preferences, and that means near-full-term fetuses do have rights. The failure of certain activists and a few politicians to see this has driven many in the pro-life movement absolutely white-hot with rage, understandably so. As such, in an attempt to force the issue, lawsuits for murder have sometimes been filed in certain legal cases where a pregnant woman has been assaulted and her fetus killed. One such case was that of a woman from my home state of Wisconsin, named Tracy Marciniak.

In 1992, Marciniak's estranged husband, Glenndale Black, assaulted her. According to reports, he brutally beat her, hit her twice in the abdomen, then refused to call 911 or let Tracy call 911. As a result, her baby died, and she was very nearly killed herself. She was only *five days* away from scheduled full term pregnancy.

Maddeningly, when she sought to press charges against Black for the manslaughter of her child, she discovered that she couldn't because Wisconsin law did not consider a fetus a human being until after it was born. Black was instead only charged with assault and wrongful imprisonment. Tracy Marciniak's plight became a landmark event which led to a change of the legal code of the State of Wisconsin in 1998, and brought about the "Unborn Victims of Violence Act" to the United States Senate and House of Representatives. On April 1st, 2004, President George W. Bush finally signed the act into law. The general public overwhelmingly agreed that birth is not the place to draw the line.

Okay, fine. But then, what about the opposite end of the spectrum? Does life begin at conception?

Upon examining the evidence, the surprising answer must be – *no!* Remember that earlier, it was pointed out that we must bow to the scientific evidence regardless of our political preferences. Here is just such an example again, as you will soon see.

Both sperm and egg are very much alive before they join together. Both mother and father are very much alive when they produce sperm and egg. The sperm and eggs which made the parents, in turn, were very much alive before they joined together, and so forth. If we are to be honest with ourselves, we must conclude that life does not begin at conception. Life begins at the dawn of all life upon Planet Earth! It has been an *unbroken* chain reaction ever since. But this is merely semantics. As the old adage goes, one gets the wrong answers if one asks the wrong questions. To avoid this technicality, we must approach the problem correctly, not by asking, "When does *life* begin?" but rather, "When does the life of an *individual being* begin?"

Okay, now we have the question accurately framed, but *when is* that point exactly? Why *not* conception?

To answer that, we must examine the fertilization scene between a sperm and ovum, as has been observed in scientists' microscopes ever since the 1840's. When sperm meets egg to form a zygote, a living thing with all the genetic material of an individual person has come into being. It has a complete and unique DNA chain, 48 chromosomes, and has begun the process which will eventually cause it to grow to adulthood—a process which it will not fully complete until 21.75 years later. (It is 21.75 instead of simply 21 because we ought to include the additional nine-month gestation period.) Based upon these facts, many conclude that an individual life does, in fact, begin at this point. And because some birth control methods work by preventing the zygote from attaching to the uterine wall, the conclusion is sometimes drawn that use of such methods are immoral.

Yet something very interesting can happen after a zygote forms. It is at this point that the cells multiply furiously, going from a few to a few hundred thousand in a very short amount of time. And here it is that the zygote, in rare but not uncommon cases, can *split* to form *two* growing zygotes to make a pair of *twins*. In much rarer cases, the zygote could split three ways to form *triplets*. So the life of a single individual simply cannot begin at the point of conception. It could be more than one after that point! In most cases, four to five *days* after that point. *Conception is logically ruled out!*.

So if an individual human life does not begin at conception, and definitely does begin before birth, then it must happen somewhere in between. Makes sense in theory, but there's quite a lot of gray area in between the two. The instantaneous reaction of a pro-lifer reading this will probably be something like, "Well, okay, but the point at which we must draw the line can't be much longer after that. In fact, it must be so soon after that point that the point at which we must draw the line is still, for all intents and purposes, conception." Well, perhaps. But what other possible criteria can be used to determine the point at which growing human cells become growing human being?

One possibility is the point at which the zygote attaches itself to the uterine wall. Drawing the line here has the benefit of being a clear milestone at which to draw a legal distinction. It also allows for the contraceptive pill, since that particular contraceptive medication works by preventing the zygote from attaching. Yet there isn't much formal difference between unattached zygote and attached embryo. The only true difference, at least at first, is a physical contact with the mother's innards. This is not insignificant, but insufficient for purposes of drawing the line for the onset of an individual life. We will see why in a moment.

Another possibility involves the measurement of vital signs. Vital signs are universally used in the medical profession to determine if a patient is alive or dead. Such vital signs would include the obvious signs of respiration and heartbeat. Respiration, of course, will not truly happen until after birth is complete, yet a fetus begins to breathe uterine fluid at around 12 weeks. The embryonic heart begins beating at only 22 days after conception. Since a heartbeat is more easily measured than fluid breathing, and is a more traditional hallmark of life, many people draw the line here. Many pregnancies are not discovered until after this point, so pretty much all abortion procedures would be declared immoral by this criteria. Not surprisingly, many of these criteria could be used as the next place to draw the legal line. In fact, many medical professionals, who know about zygotes and twins, and who happen to be pro-life themselves, use one or more of these points in their own personal philosophy!

The problem with these is that each one of them is arbitrary, and medical science has already made them obsolete. Defining a living being by heartbeat, for example, gets interesting in the case of a cardiac patient who is given a mechanical heart. Such a patient might be considered someone who is not truly a living being, because there is no true heartbeat. (A Jarvic-7 might have an actual beat, but other mechanical heart devices might do nothing more than hum softly.) But this argument is clearly silly. The person is obviously alive, and one can talk and interact with her freely. A similar situation could arise when a patient with failed lungs or no lungs at all is hooked up to a machine which aerates the blood. Such a patient would have no breath to speak of (or with), but would still be obviously alive. Medical technology further complicates the issue by the use of transplants. If a patient is given a heart from a different body, does that mean that patient has been given someone *else's* life? Perhaps in a sense that's true, but not actually, because the life of the donor was already ended by some other malady. This is why those who display the popular bumper sticker, "Abortion stops a beating heart," are completely missing the point. Heartbeat and respiration are vital *signs*, but not the vitality itself! They are not what defines a separate being, and thus arguments which cite them are moot. Neither a beating heart nor a breathing lung necessarily define an individual. A better place to draw the line is needed.

Such a line exists. There is one other vital sign which greatly outweighs heartbeat and respiration. That vital sign is *brain activity*.

1. The Brain

Of course! It makes the most sense. When someone is alive, it means the *brain* is alive. When someone is dead, it can only mean *brain* dead! All other signs of life are negotiable, but once the brain is gone, that's it! Every organ in your body, except one, can be replaced with a donor organ or a mechanical device, and you would still be "you," fundamentally speaking. The one organ that cannot be replaced, and in fact can *never* be replaced, is your *brain*. Without a brain, a person simply isn't there. This is why if a patient is "brain dead," that we must heartbreakingly pull the plug on the life support machine. In fact, a living body with a dead brain is bluntly referred to as a "beating-heart cadaver" in the medical profession, particularly among surgeons eager to harvest the organs for transplant. If a patient is not quite brain-dead, but merely in a coma (and sometimes it is frustratingly hard to tell the difference), the decision on whether or not to disconnect the life support becomes much more difficult. That debate itself could be the subject of a whole different book. But for now, we can establish one thing with absolute certainty: The *brain* defines the being.

To illustrate, we can do a little "thought experiment." Let's take a not-so-voluntary imaginary test subject, and just for fun, let's make it Jerry Falwell. (As the late Rev. Falwell has already passed on, I'm sure he won't mind. But for our discussion, we'll pretend he's still alive.) First, we'll surgically remove Jerry's brain from his body (don't worry, we'll put it back when we're done) and we'll then place his body on artificial life support so that it doesn't get any more putrefied than it already is. (All right now, no joking about his small brain size, that's just not nice!) Next, we'll place his brain into a very sophisticated, computerized robot, capable not only of sustaining Jerry's brain, but also interacting with it, so that he'll be able to control the robot from inside. (True, this kind of advanced technology is still only science fiction for now, but it's useful for thinking about the issue anyway.) Once this process is complete, the robot will be able to jump to life and, in an electronic-sounding voice, say things like, *"Hillary Clinton is Satan! Vote Republican! Tithe, and you will prosper!"*

Now, here's the kicker question: Where is (for want of a better word) Mr. Fallwell's *soul?* Where is his *spirit?* Where is the ontological *being* that makes up Jerry Falwell?

If you said, 'Inside the robot,' you'd be exactly right! Where *else* could it be? His body may be lying on a hospital bed, but Falwell *himself* is elsewhere. For all functional purposes, the robot is now the Reverend Falwell! The *brain* defines the being. Not the body.

Keep in mind, Jerry's body exhibits all the indications of life, what medical professionals refer to as, "vital signs." Although kept going by artificial means, it's breathing is still taking place, it's heart is still beating, it's circulatory and nervous systems are all fully formed (that is, the nervous system sans the brain, which is technically part of the nervous system), and its immune system is still working. It has all the qualities of a developing fetus – with the exception that it is growing old instead of up.

And here's where it *really* gets interesting: Suppose we were to unplug the life support system, and let Jerry's body die. (That would be very mean of us, but it's merely a thought-experiment anyway.) Have we then committed murder? To be sure, we've killed the body, which makes us guilty of destruction of property at the very least, but have we killed Jerry *himself?*

The clear answer is *no!* As heinous as our act is, as brutal as it is, and whatever else our crime may be, it's not murder because Jerry's brain is still alive, albeit bodiless. His brain, still inside the robot, is capable of hiring a lawyer and *suing* us for killing his body!

What he can't sue us for, is *murder.* Jerry, you see, is still alive!

But if *that's* true, what about the killing of a fetus with a brain which has not yet formed?

If you're pro-life, the question isn't so simple anymore, is it?

I once explored this theme in a short science fiction story I once wrote entitled, *The Trial of Avery Froelich* (Bastion Science Fiction Magazine, April 2014) in which a murder victim's brain survives inside a robotic life-support system, just like I've described above. (I've included it as an appendix at the end of this book.) Because abortion and euthanasia were both outlawed in my story's setting (which was the planet Mars), the brain did not determine his status of life or death under the law. Thus, the victim was technically dead, even though his brain was still alive. He was able to testify, in person, at *his own* murder trial! A beautiful illustration of the absurdity of not letting the brain define the being!

In our mind's eye, let's put Robertson's brain back, and apply the knowledge we've gained from this to fetal development. We need to ask ourselves, at what point does a growing fetus become a growing being? Or, to put it in religious terms, at what point of development does the *soul* and/or *spirit* enter the body? The answer should be obvious. The being forms when the *brain* forms. Without a developed brain, there is no house for either soul or spirit. Or, as a gentleman from the South once phrased it for me, "Can't carry no water if there ain't nothin' to pour it into."

Suppose, for a moment, that a "conceptionist" (my poor invention of a word for someone who espouses the *personhood* doctrine – the belief that the life of an individual begins at conception rather than brain formation) disagreed with this. If such a person insists that a soul enters the body at conception, and we return to our earlier example of identical twins, what has happened? Does each twin get only *half* a soul? Or do *two* souls enter only one zygote before twins form? Such possibilities seem absurd. Any soul must *first* have a brain before it can interact with a body.

I have often heard the argument: "Obviously, God put two souls into the zygote. That's why it split to become twins in the first place!" But this is assuming things without evidence. It also assumes that zygotes *can* hold souls, and as we've seen, without a brain, they clearly can't! One could argue that God intended to place two souls into two bodies, and thus the zygote split into two, but if so, the vessels into which God would pour these souls (i.e., the brains) wouldn't form until much later.

Of course, that doesn't really settle the issue. Far from it! Spiritual arguments can find any excuse they wish to against physical evidence. Also, the brain forms *gradually*, denying us of any obvious milestone at which to draw a hard line. But perhaps by understanding the process of brain formation, we can find an applicable solution to the issue. How does a brain form?

The very earliest any brain activity becomes detectable, as acknowledged even by pro-life publications, is just barely less than six weeks.[2] A fetus begins to move a little at around 7 weeks of development, demonstrating that the brain stem forms rather quickly, as does the *cerebellum*, the center of movement and coordination. Until that point, it's pretty stationary. Movement remains fairly limited up until around 9 weeks. Then, by 10 weeks, something very interesting happens. The fetus begins to move quite a bit! It jumps, kicks, punches and twists, demonstrating that the cerebellum is "wired" and has initiated its full "systems check." When viewed by ultrasound, it makes for some compelling video. Many pro-life videos feature such ultrasounds prominently in their circulated media. Interestingly, this movement cannot be felt by the mother just yet, but that's rather trivial in the overall grand scheme of things. In the meantime, the bottom line is that 10 weeks marks the point at which the developing fetus begins any significant movement. We can call this milestone, "physical quickening." The earlier point of six weeks would mark the point of earliest brain activity.

Are either of *these* a good place where we should draw the line?

The idea has a certain amount of appeal, but it satisfies very few people. On the pro-choice side, some of the most necessary abortions tend to occur after these stages, either because of fear of reprisal by family and church, being ethically conflicted and so putting the decision off, feeling guilty over the (in some cases) rape or incest which brought the pregnancy about, or even worse, not having the procedure done in a more timely manner due to lack of money. Since only 16% of abortions are performed at or prior to six weeks, the vast majority of abortions would be ruled out. On the pro-life side, drawing the line at ten weeks of development means that the vast majority of abortions would happen anyway. Depending on your statistician, the number of abortions done prior to ten weeks ranges from 73% to 88%. (A key pro-life publication says 77%.[3]) Part of the confusion arises over the point at which one begins reckoning the pregnancy. A pro-life advocate will sometimes tally development beginning from the point of conception, while a pro-choice advocate will reckon development beginning from the date of a woman's last menstrual period (LMP), causing a variance as high

---

[2] Specifically, 40 days. *Pro Life Answers to Pro Choice Arguments*, p. 67, Randy Alcorn, Multnomah Publications, Sisters, Oregon, 1992.
[3] *Ibid.*

as 2-3 weeks. Sometimes, it's the other way around. Which tally is used often depends upon which political side of the argument one is on, or even upon what point, specifically, is trying to be made.

What a confusing mess! For all the problems that exist when drawing the line at conception, it's at least a simple milestone. It seems that there ought to be a much better place to draw the line, either before or after six to ten weeks' gestation. As it turns out, there is, and it has to do with the development of the brain again. This time, we deal with, not the cerebellum, the center of movement, but with the *cerebrum*, the center of reasoning.

The cerebrum is the upper part of the brain, comprising most of its mass. When people think of a brain, they tend to think of the crinkled surface divided into two halves which is basically what the cerebrum is. All higher thought processes are done there. The underlying parts of the brain, such as the pons, medulla oblongata, midbrain, and the aforementioned cerebellum, play little role in conscious thought. If there is a seat of consciousness, if there is a "house for the soul," it is here.

To illustrate, let us again snag our convenient imaginary test subject, Jerry Falwell. We again surgically remove his brain from his body, but *this* time, we do it a little bit differently. This time, we remove his cerebrum only, while leaving his *brain stem* behind, a process which in medical terms is known as *decerebration*. We place Jerry's cerebrum into the robot, just as before, and once again, the robot rears its head and asks what the heck it's doing back inside this newfangled machine. But Jerry's body needn't be placed on life support this time. *This* time, his body is able to sustain itself *on its own*, and exhibits some very unique qualities.

We know from decerebrating laboratory animals what happens in such cases. Cats and dogs often exhibit behavior which give all the appearance of being willed by a conscious mind, despite having no mind there. Decerebrate cats, if dropped upside-down from sufficient height, will land on their feet, as cats are wont to do, and decerebrate dogs will right themselves if pushed off balance.[4] Decerebrate birds will fly, land on a branch, and remain balanced in

---

[4] Sherrington, Sir Charles, *Man on his Nature*, Cambridge University Press, 1963, pp. 35 & 149f.

a perching position.[5] Yet these animals are, essentially, mindless. Once righted, and standing, the animal will do little else.

And *Jerry's* body? It will be able to walk if led about, will respond to sounds, will react to pain, and will show periods of apparent sleeping and wakefulness—all traits which are well beyond that which is apparent in a late-developing embryo or fetus. For all intents and purposes, the Rev. Falwell appears to be within his body, but in a kind of trance. But in point of fact, his body is "mindless." It's a little like – no, on second thought, it's *exactly* like – Falwell's ship no longer has a captain or crew to sail with. Falwell *himself* (his Captain Consciousness, if you will) is within the mechanized machine we placed his cerebrum in earlier! He is less passionate this time because his thinking brain is disconnected from the emotional centers, such as the amygdala, but he's there. It is this robotic machine which will voice electronic-sounding objections to our having placed him inside there in the first place—perhaps as un-emotionally as a Vulcan from Star Trek. It will be the *robot* which will espouse his political opinions and speak in favor of conservative candidates. And it is the robot who will telephone his lawyers if we do not put his cerebrum back into his body straightaway. Indeed, if we failed to put his cerebrum back soon, his body would probably die in a couple of weeks, the way all decerebrate animals do.

Meanwhile, inside the robot, Jerry's brain will still be capable of thought and reasoning, but this time, it will be divorced from his animal passions. He will feel no fear, no anxiety, no sadness, no happiness, no sexual attraction to young and pretty women (though some may argue he never had that to begin with). Essentially, he will be every bit as emotionless as Star Trek's android character, Data.

But suppose we *didn't* put Jerry's cerebrum back? Suppose we again let Jerry's body die? *Now* would we have committed *murder?* Would it be murder if we killed a fetus whose cerebrum had not yet developed?

Again, not so simple if you're pro-life, is it?

---

[5] Carlson, A.J., and Johnson, V., *The Machinery of the Body*, University of Chicago Press, 1941, p. 422. Also, Walter S. Cannon, *The Way of an Investigator*, Hafner, New York, 1968 (reprint), p. 121.

Jerry's *body* exhibits all the vital signs of a living being. Heartbeat, respiration, movement—all indicate a living being. Yet the "being" is *absent!* The *mind* is gone, and with it, the soul/spirit. We now take that mind/soul/spirit out of the robot and put it back into Jerry's body with no further thought of doing him any more mischief today. But although this was merely a "thought experiment," the lesson has been learned. No amount of movement, reaction to pain, or level of physical development can show that a fetus has crossed the threshold from living human *cells* to living human *being*.

What *does* show this, is the level of development of the *cerebrum*. We must then ask, at what point does the *cerebrum* develop?

The cerebrum doesn't begin to develop until at least the *20th week* of a woman's pregnancy. This is the earliest known point at which we have any scientific evidence at all that the fetus can be *conscious* of feeling pain. And just what liberal, left-wing publication did *that* bit of information come from? Why, it came from the newsletter of the National Right to Life Committee![6] That's right folks, the pro-lifers have known all along when consciousness begins! Translation: The "soul" does not enter the body until, at the very earliest, the fifth month of a development, or the exact *half-way point* of a woman's pregnancy.

It is at 20 weeks that the cerebral cortex *begins* to be "fully wired." It is at this point that electroencephalographs (EEG's) reveal the sudden appearance of the first true alpha, beta, gamma and theta "brain waves."[7] It is only slightly before this point that a sudden growth spurt in the cerebrum takes place.

Interestingly, this is also the earliest point at which a mother first feels her baby moving inside her. Now *that's* an odd coincidence, isn't it? It is almost as if the Creator God were trying to tell us something. Perhaps that message is that the line should be drawn when the mother *feels* her baby move! (In fact, many theologians have drawn the line *exactly* there in the past.)

---

[6] Ranalli, Paul, M.D., "A Pain Too Awful to Imagine," National Right to Life News, April 2004, p. 13.

[7] Anand, K.J., Hickey, P.R., "Pain and its effects on the human neonate and fetus," New England Journal of Medicine, 317:1321-1329, Nov. 19, 1987.

Is this, then, where we can safely draw the line? Certainly, the half-way point is a clear-cut marker that is easy to remember, but that advantage is hardly a solid reason to draw the line there. 20 weeks may be the very earliest point at which the cerebrum begins to function, but is it fairly and objectively refer to as, "mental quickening?"

Pro-life politicians have certainly seemed to think so. In 2015, the Republican-led congress introduced H.R. 36 – the Pain-Capable Unborn Child Protection Act. It was a bill designed to outlaw abortion at 20 weeks into a woman's pregnancy on the grounds that this was the earliest point at which a fetus could feel pain. It was part of a national trend that year which saw 20-week abortion bans enacted (at the time of this writing) by state legislatures in 17 states. (Alabama, Arizona, Arkansas, Georgia, Idaho, Indiana, Kansas, Louisiana, Mississippi, Nebraska, North Carolina, North Dakota, Ohio, Oklahoma, Texas, West Virginia and Wisconsin. Three of these, in Arizona, Georgia and Idaho, were struck down.) During debate on the House floor, Rep. Ralph Abraham, Republican from Louisiana, famously said:

> "As a doctor, I know and I can attest that this bill is backed by scientific research showing that babies can indeed feel pain at 20 weeks, if not before."

But what these politicians unwittingly did was draw the line somewhere *else* besides conception. In other words, they publicly *admitted* that conception was not the place to draw the line, and argued instead that the developmental point at which a fetus could first feel pain was more reasonable!

Of course, that's not the way those on the pro-life side saw it. In their view, anything which outlawed some abortions was a victory of sorts, and was part of an overall strategy to make abortion illegal by taking it down one small piece at a time – a "death by 1,000 paper-cuts" approach. But this time, the strategy backfired, and made the entire position vulnerable to a sensible counter-attack (based in large part by the arguments presented here in this book[8]). The

---

[8] The fact that such a counterattack did not come swiftly and starkly was a source of intense frustration to me. Why, when the enemy has exposed it's vulnerable flank, would you not charge? The failure of NARAL and other pro-choice groups to act on this – indeed, to act *at all* – is one reason this book exists.

argument that conception is where an individual life begins will never again be respected in the same way, or by the same number of people.

As if the 20-week gaff wasn't bad enough, it was also flat-out *wrong*. A fetus does *not* begin to feel pain at 20 weeks! It begins to feel pain *much* later. A synthesis of evidence regarding this was published in *JAMA* (the Journal of the American Medical Association) back in 2005, almost a full decade before Republicans began pushing for 20-week ban on Capitol Hill. It brought together experts from the University of California, San Francisco, and elsewhere, and their report concluded: "Evidence regarding the capacity for fetal pain is limited but indicates that fetal perception of pain is unlikely before the third trimester."[9] A pregnancy takes 36 weeks (roughly 9 months) from point of conception. Doctors estimate 40 weeks from a woman's last menstrual period (LMP) because that's easier to quantify as a measure. So the point at which a fetus can feel pain is between 24 to 28 weeks, depending on your measuring methods. That pushes the mean value of the "point of ensoulment," that is, "mental quickening," or more bluntly, the beginning point of an individual's life, out to roughly *26 weeks* into the clinical definition of a woman's pregnancy, or *one and a half months* after the cutoff point in the Pain-Capable Unborn Child Protection Act of 2015.

A March 2010 report from the Royal College of Obstetricians and Gynaecologists in the United Kingdom concluded similarly, saying, "In reviewing the neuroanatomical and physiological evidence in the fetus, it was apparent that connections from the periphery to the cortex are not intact before 24 weeks of gestation and, as most neuroscientists believe that the cortex is necessary for pain perception, it can be concluded that the fetus cannot experience pain in any sense prior to this gestation."[10] In 2012, the American Congress of Obstetricians and Gynecologists agreed with these findings, writing that "[s]upporters of fetal pain legislation only present studies which support the claim of fetal pain

---

[9] *JAMA*, August 24-31, 2005, Vol. 294, No. 8., pp 947-954.
[10]

https://www.rcog.org.uk/globalassets/documents/guidelines/rcogfetalawarenesswp r0610.pdf prior to the third trimester. When weighed together with other available information, including the JAMA and RCOG studies, supporters' conclusion does not stand."[11]

To put it in layman's terms, the cerebellum *may* fully form by 20 weeks, but it has yet to be "plugged in" to the cerebrum, and until it is, there is no sensory input, no pain reception, and consequentially, no start to an individual's conscious life.

And this is why politicians should not draft laws on medicine without being schooled by medical professionals first.

After inadvertently blowing up their entire argument, the *Pain-Capable Unborn Child Protection Act* failed in the Senate on Sept. 22, 2015. They had enough votes to pass, but not enough to prevent a Democratic filibuster. To add even more salt to this wound, it was all pointless, as President Barack Obama would have vetoed the bill anyway.

So there it finally is! The point at which living, growing human cells cross over into becoming a living, growing human being is 24-28 weeks, or just after the start of the third trimester. In spiritual terms, this is really the only logical point at which the "soul" can reasonably be considered to "enter the body." It is *here* that we should rightly draw the line, one which we could accurately call the "line of ensoulment."

When scientists first began serious study of the brain, one of the first things that they looked for was the seat of the soul – that part of the brain which was thought to be the center of conscious being, which sees through the video cameras of the eyes and hears through the audio relays of the ears, operating the human body much the same way as a construction worker operates the controls of a large machine – the *homunculus*, as this is sometimes called. But the more they searched, the more they found that there didn't seem to be any particular central point of consciousness. Rene Descartes, the famous mathematician, once bizarrely postulated that the *pineal gland* might be this center. He was refuted on this by Baruch Spinoza and others. As medical knowledge accumulated, it became

---

[11] ACOG Statement On HR 3803, District of Columbia Pain-Capable Unborn Child Protection Act, June 18, 2012.
http://www.acog.org/~/media/Departments/Government%20Relations%20and%20 Outreach/20120618DCAborStmnt.pdf

clear that the brain seemed to operate more or less as a whole, and the homunculus idea had to be given up. For the abortion debate, this is rather unfortunate, because it means that there's no exact lobe in a brain we can point to and say, "Aha! At *this* point, the being has developed, and there is definitely a soul inside the fetus!" But we don't need one. It is when the brain as a whole forms sufficiently that we may point to it and say, "Now it has crossed the threshold. Now it has rights."

But why should someone who respects the sanctity of life accept the rationale behind this argument? After all, a fetus is *alive* before its brain forms, isn't it?

For the answer to that, we must look to Chapter 3. But first, we need to take an important digression.

2. Abortion Theology

This was originally intended to be the final chapter, and in a perfect world, it would be. I could let my rational arguments lead the way, and then leave the final chapter as a clean-up job for any who might still object on the basis of "God said so." But let's face it, religious belief is at the heart of much anti-abortion sentiment, and those who object the strongest do so first and foremost because they believe they are doing the will of the Almighty. Because of that, we need to look at the theological arguments first, and thus, hopefully, free up the minds of readers to more scientific arguments later. Early on, I pointed out that abortion being murder was decided by *clergy,* and does not stem from any claim to direct revelation from God. But in the absence of any direct memo from On High, how does one divine *God's* will on the abortion issue?

One way is to look at nature. It's an old idea: the way to know God is to understand His creation. In other words, the maker is known through his handiwork. We can therefore observe nature, and from it, perhaps obtain a glimpse into the nature of the Almighty Himself. It is attested by virtually every Christian pro-lifer, that God is the designer of all life. Yet according to that design, 15-20% of all recognized pregnancies end in miscarriage. Usually a miscarriage happens before 12 weeks of development, but it can sometimes happen up until the 20th week of pregnancy, which is roughly the half-way point. But the 15-20% is only a percentage of *recognized* pregnancies, meaning those that the medical profession are made aware of. Some figures indicate that as many as *50%* of total pregnancies end in miscarriage! Most websites which console women over their miscarriages repeat these same numbers. Yet the medical term for a miscarriage is *spontaneous abortion.* The question then becomes, if God is the designer of all life, why did he design women to undergo so very many spontaneous abortions *naturally?*

An evangelical theologian would be quick to point out that, according to Christian eschatology, it is *Satan,* not God, who is the bringer of death. But who made Satan? Who allowed, and still allows, him to work? Who let him into the Garden of Eden? Who let him tempt Eve? Casting Satan as the progenitor of miscarriage does not absolve God on this issue. The Bible even clearly states that not one sparrow will fall to the ground without the will of God the Father, and that humans are worth much more than sparrows (Matthew 10:29-31). We can therefore conclude from scripture that dying sparrows and spontaneous abortions both happen by God's will. When a doctor at a clinic performs an abortion procedure, he or she is merely following the lead of Almighty Father, the Divine Abortionist.

But this is almost too simple, and few will be swayed by it. Is there more? Indeed there is! Abortion, whether it's a miscarriage or done by human means, is only *physical* death. Remember, according to Christian teaching, those who reject Christ suffer eternal torment. I wonder, just how many souls rejected Christianity and thus qualified for Hell's flames because they had a philosophical problem with fundamentalists' stubborn insistence on being anti-abortion? And if one believes fetuses *have* souls prior to 20 weeks, don't the souls of those aborted fetuses go *straight to heaven?* Isn't abortion doing the unborn a *favor?* Allowing a baby to be born is putting its soul through a needless and unnecessary risk! And abortion doctors are actually the most successful soul-winners in God's arsenal against cheating Satan!

Am I being facetious? A little, yes. Yet logically, the point is still hilariously sound. Here lies, perhaps, the ultimate irony in Christian opposition to abortion: In order to save the lives of millions of unborn babies, they end up losing a large percentage of their *souls* to the eternal flames of hellfire. They will have saved them physically, only to lose them spiritually – which to a true Christian is supposedly far, far worse a fate. Can Pat Robertson, Jerry Falwell, Randall Terry,[12] Matt Trewhella,[13] Wanda Franz[14] and their like, truly face their Father in Heaven, having lost so many millions of souls so Satan's Abyss, and not be ashamed? Can they face this fact knowing that they put so many young girls through their own private hell in order to do it?

Hmmm… Just *where* was this "modern-day holocaust" taking place again?

---

[12] Founder of Operation Rescue.
[13] Leader of Missionaries to the Preborn.
[14] President of the National Right to Life Committee.

Earlier, it was pointed out how scripture had nothing to say on the subject of abortion. But this is not entirely true. It is more accurate to say that the Bible has nothing to say *against* abortion, and it does have a few things to say, by inference, about the sanctity of a baby's life – both prior to, and after, birth. The most interesting example of this is found in Numbers chapter 5, verses 11-31, where, if a husband suspects his wife has been cheating on him, he can bring her to the Jewish temple where the priest will make up a potion made up of holy water, dust from the temple floor and the washed-off ink of scrolls containing curses, and give it to the suspected wife to drink.

> "27 If she has made herself impure and been unfaithful to her husband, this will be the result: When she is made to drink the water that brings a curse and causes bitter suffering, it will enter her, her abdomen will swell and her womb will miscarry, and she will become a curse. 28 If, however, the woman has not made herself impure, but is clean, she will be cleared of guilt and will be able to have children."

At first glance, this passage seems quite clear. God's priest induces a miscarriage for a wife's infidelity. In other words, priests of the temple of David and Solomon induced abortions!

Of course, Bible scholars are quick to counter this one! They quickly quote the more traditional King James Version, which reads this way:

> "27 And when he hath made her to drink the water, then it shall come to pass, that, if she be defiled, and have done trespass against her husband, that the water that causeth the curse shall enter into her, and become bitter, and her belly shall swell, and her thigh shall rot: and the woman shall be a curse among her people.
> "28 And if the woman be not defiled, but be clean; then she shall be free, and shall conceive seed."

Now, in our modern English vernacular, the words, "her thigh shall rot" sounds rather innocent, and plenty of pro-choice ministers are anxious to say that this does not necessarily mean a miscarriage, and that therefore this passage is not an endorsement of abortion. But these men of the cloth are quite mistaken. First, verse 28 clearly says that if the woman is innocent, she "shall conceive

27

seed," meaning that she will not be barren. Thus, the strong implication is that the previous verse indicates that she *will* be barren if she is guilty. If she is barren, then she will not give birth, and that means miscarriage, no matter which way you spin it. Also, (and this is not well known outside of some very intense Bible scholars), the word "thigh" is often used as a euphemism for a person's genitals. For example, in Genesis 24:2, Abraham makes his servant swear an oath by having him place his hand under his "thigh." But that's not what the text means. He is having his servant touch his most intimate parts in order to bind him in the strongest possible way to a most secretive oath. So in Numbers, when it says that the woman's "thigh shall rot," it plainly means her uterus.

It helps to understand how the New International Version was created. In a committee of various scholars from many different denominations, it was collectively discussed, and then voted upon, how to phrase many of the Bible's more difficult passages in English. If there was any chance to smooth over or obfuscate theological problems in the process, they would have had the opportunity to do so. But here, in this key passage from Numbers, it bluntly says "miscarriage." They did *not* do this because they were trying to be pro-choice! They phrased it this way because they knew there was no way around it. True, the Hebrew word for "miscarry" (*shakal*) was not used, but it did not have to be.

Now, the purpose of this ritual as described in the book of Numbers was probably not to actually cause abortions. Certainly, the Jewish priesthood was not actually doing abortions in the Holy Temple! Rather, the ritual was designed to scare a cheating woman into confessing her sin. Floor dust and a little scribe's ink would not be enough for any woman to spontaneously miscarry a stillborn fetus onto the floor. But standing in front of a priest who had, in the woman's eyes, the power of the Lord God Himself, and being threatened with a very frightening curse if she were to be guilty, might be enough to cause her to confess her sin of infidelity, and maybe even a few more sins besides! So why didn't the scriptures clarify this? Well, if it did, the cat would be out of the bag, wouldn't it? So the authors of Numbers described the ritual, but left out *why* the ritual was really there – as an interrogation tool to be used by the priesthood to elicit confessions from unfaithful wives.

Here's another scripture: The most famous example of God's extermination of the preborn might be Noah's flood. Quick recap: God informs Noah that all humanity has grown so wicked that he will wipe the planet clean of the entire species in a great, world-wide flood. But because Noah and his family are righteous, they will be saved. He is told to build an ark, which will hold himself, his family, and at least two of every kind of beastie on Earth. Under ridicule, he builds the gigantic boat. But the laughter subsides as the animals arrive and the rain begins to fall. Noah shuts the door, turning a deaf ear to the screams and pleadings of the people who subsequently drown.

Now, putting aside the ethics of a God who hauls off and smites the whole world out of sheer spite in this way, there lies within this legendary story a weighty implication in the abortion debate. The flood destroyed an entire human population, if one takes the story to be historical. That means about half the population were women, and probably about one quarter of those women were of child-bearing age. Without question, with all the wrath-incurring immorality going around, a percentage of those women would have been pregnant at the time of the flood. Yet God drowned them, mother and unborn baby alike, at a single stroke. Amazing how the Almighty had such callous disregard for the rights of innocent children and the preborn!

The flood of Noah is one of the most prominent Sunday-school lessons of all time. Every Christian child learns it young, and every moon-bat creationist tries using it as the explanation for ancient geologic features such as the Grand Canyon, or the Great Rift valley in Africa. Yet present within that very story was a theological lesson with shattering political implications in the abortion debate – and it was there in plain sight all the time. God had little or no regard for preborn rights when he sent the flood. He made no provision for innocent children, born or unborn, to be saved. It could be argued that God somehow rendered women infertile in the months or years leading up to the flood, but the text simply doesn't say that, and its absence speaks volumes.

But there are plenty of other scriptures that show the God of the Old Testament completely disregards the innocence of children. When Sodom and Gomorrah were found to be wicked, God destroyed the cities with fire and brimstone. Only Abraham's nephew Lot and his family were saved. But again, it stands to reason that these city populations had some pregnant women and children in tow. Were they saved? Did God whisk them away? No. Just like in Noah's flood, they were killed too.

In that story, Abraham haggles with God until the Lord says that he will spare the city if only 10 righteous men are found within it. Abraham might have won his case had he told the Almighty to include the *fetuses* within the city!

Yet again God kills all the firstborn children in Egypt as the tenth plague. Not that the *children* ever did anybody any harm! The just thing to do would have been to strike down Pharaoh, since he was the stubborn guy who refused to let the Israelites go. But God apparently considers children fodder for making a strong point.

Another of the most memorable Bible stories is that of Abraham and Isaac. After granting Abraham the miracle of a son in his wife's old age, God commands him to sacrifice that son to him as a burnt offering. Astonishingly, he actually *agrees* to this! God watches Abraham being obedient to this insanity all the way up until he raises the knife and is about to plunge it down into his son's body. Then and only then does God stop him. Okay, true, the Almighty relented, but just what kind of a twisted mind conceives of such a sick test of loyalty? Did he not care about the psychological trauma forever visited upon Isaac?

Primary point: If God demanded the sacrifice of Isaac as a young boy at least several years of age, what does that say about the attitude He must have toward the *unborn?*

Then there are the slaughters of the Israelites. Again and again, the Israelites are depicted as slaughtering the people and cities of the Canaanites, "men, women and children." (The Bible's words, not mine.[15]) In many cases, even the livestock were slaughtered. Most Christians read the story of the fall of the walls of Jericho and take from it a story of unflappable faith. The Veggie Tales franchise even made a funny kids' video about it. The part where the Israelites slaughter all the innocent *children* afterward is glossed over or outright omitted. Few Sunday Schools teach about the Israelite slaughter of the Midianites (Numbers Ch. 31), in which God,

---

[15] Numbers 31:13-18; Deuteronomy 2:33-34; Deuteronomy 20:13-17; Joshua 6:21; 1 Samuel 15:3-8.

through Moses, directly ordered that all the young boys, and every woman who had slept with a man should be killed. The virgin girls were to be kept as booty for the victorious army. So how does one tell if a woman has slept with a man? A broken hymen is traditional, but not perfect. It's fairly easy to tell if the woman is older. But what about the young women? Well, a swollen, distended *pregnant* belly is a dead giveaway! Thus, at God's order, these pregnant women, according to the Bible, were put to the sword – a blatantly not-so-partial-birth abortion!

But the crown jewel of Bible stories, at least from a pro-choice standpoint, is the story of David and Bathsheba. When King David lusted after the beautiful Bathsheba, he wasted no time in sleeping with her, despite the fact that she was already married. When she became pregnant, a dilemma presented itself which any modern teenage girl can relate to. David's solution to the dilemma was to order that Bathsheba's husband, Uriah the Hittite, be placed at the front of the line in battle and then left exposed to enemy fire. Naturally, he got killed, and David wasted no time in marrying the widow. Dilemma solved, right?

Well, wrong. The prophet Nathan learned of this, and confronted David. When David repented (fat lot of good that did at *that* point!) Nathan declared the Lord's judgment upon the king. As punishment for David's sin, the firstborn child of he and Bathsheba would die. Then David would be forgiven. Sure enough, the child fell ill after birth. Despite all David's pleading and praying for the child's life to be spared, it soon died. God's will be done.

But wait a minute! Look at this story a bit closer. Daddy sinned, so the *baby* had to die?! Is this not pro-abortion thinking in its purest form? Indeed it is! Judeo-Christians who say that killing a baby to deal with a pregnancy conceived in sin is contrary to God's will need to re-examine Heavenly Father's track record! Perhaps Jesus said it best when he said, "*Suffer* the little children."

There are a few other examples, and not all of them involve the brutal slaughter of innocent children or women carrying unborn children. For example, in Exodus 21:22-23, the Law of Moses describes what to do if two men fight and cause a woman to miscarry.

"If people are fighting and hit a pregnant woman and she gives birth prematurely but there is no serious injury, the offender must be fined whatever the woman's husband demands and the court allows."

The implication is, of course, that a miscarried fetus is not considered serious injury. It is not a life, but punishable with a fine only.

"But wait!" say the pro-life scriptural apologists. Perhaps this interpretation is wrong. Perhaps the premature birth is only just that – a premature birth – and the baby lives." Well, true, this interpretation is a possibility. But it's on shaky ground, especially when one considers all the examples of gratuitous slaughter of both born and unborn children, by God Himself, as cited above! Such a deity is not likely to care about any child, much less an unborn one. And the scripture in Exodus merely describes what is to be done in the event of a premature birth. It only tells what should be done if two *men* fight and cause a woman to miscarry. It doesn't bother to describe what is to be done if *one* man causes a woman to miscarry. It doesn't think it necessary to recommend a course of action if another *woman* causes the miscarriage. It doesn't bother to specify how *far along* the miscarrying woman has been pregnant. In fact, it doesn't even bother to say whether the prematurely born baby lives or dies! Why were such crucial details omitted? There can be only one answer. In the bronze-age culture that penned this rule, such details weren't important. Only men's rights mattered. And if the prematurely born baby didn't survive, well, babies died all the time, didn't they? For that matter, miscarriages happened all the time. Besides, the woman can simply get pregnant with another one. No harm, no foul. Why would a shepherding, nomadic tribal society male think any differently?

Of course, those who are not caught up in Christian dogma or Biblical literalism simply don't have to deal with the above dilemmas. In fact, the whole thing seems rather silly. Certainly, one doesn't need to be a Christian to be anti-abortion! There are certainly plenty of Hindus, Buddhists, Pagans, and even atheists and agnostics who oppose it. But for those anti-abortionists who happen to be Christian (and in America, most are), there exists a very serious piper who needs to be paid for this particular dance. God clearly aborts babies, both in natural miscarriages and within the Bible. Many people avoid Christianity because of clerical positions on abortion, and the souls of aborted fetuses are, by Christian rules, guaranteed their admission into Heaven. From the Christian perspective, anything—*anything*—which drives souls away from Jesus, should be flatly rejected. This *especially* includes the anti-abortion movement!

All this would be quite enough, but there's more. Did you know that for much of Christian history, conception was not considered the origin of a human life? Many early Church fathers considered the taking of fetal life to be wrong. Such opinions can be found in the writings of men like Clement of Alexandria (150 – 215 C.E.), Tertullian and St. Jerome (342 – 420 C.E.). But there are other contrary opinions which surfaced. The most prominent of these is St. Augustine (354 – 430 C.E.) , who condemned abortion, but considered the point of beginning of an individual life, or *hominization*, to be *after* conception. The doctrine was referred to as *"fetus animatus,"* or the point at which a fetus moves (or, *"quickening,"* as we previously called it). Since a woman cannot feel such movement until 4.5 months in, this is where many early Christian scholars drew the line. That translates to roughly 20 weeks after conception, or *24 weeks* after last menstrual period! Note that this is almost *exactly* where the earlier chapters in this book reasoned that the line should be drawn! The reasons are different, but the conclusion is the same.

The doctrine of *fetus animatus* held sway over much of Christian doctrine, and influenced the rulings of many popes, such as Innocent III (1161 – 1216 C.E.), who stated that the soul enters a fetus at the point of "quickening" (again, 24 weeks). But later popes reversed this opinion. Nevertheless, the idea took hold, and often held sway among the educated of Europe. William Blackstone (1723-1780), a justice and legal scholar from England, made the *point of quickening* the legal point at which a woman's fetus obtains rights. This idea, in turn, was the legal definition at the time of the ratification of the Constitution of the United States.

In other words, Roe v. Wade didn't take away the original law of the land. It *restored* it!

Periodically, a religion will take a position contrary to its traditions for the sake of political expediency. For example, Mormonism originally rejected polygamy. Then, to keep its central captains loyal, it adopted the practice, rewarding their primary male leaders with extra women. Later, when this proved detrimental to the

Mormon Church's interests politically, it found a theological rationale to reject the practice once again, (though a few rare pockets of Mormons still have men with multiple wives in violation of generally accepted dogma).

In like manner, the Koran clearly and unambiguously condemns suicide (Koran, Surah 4:29-30), as does the Hadith, which states that anyone who commits suicide by hanging will be hanging himself for all eternity, just as one who stabs himself will be stabbing himself in hell for all eternity. By this logic, one might think that would mean that one who blows himself up would have to blow himself up for all eternity in hell. But the Islamists have adjusted themselves, and their doctrine, to allow for terrorism. It is reasoned that if the act of suicide takes out many infidels, it then becomes a warrior's death, and not a true suicide. Yet this is proving politically detrimental to the advancement of Islam as well, making it appear quite evil. Muslim leaders around the world are beginning to make it the official dogma of their faith to reject suicide bombing as contrary to Allah's will. Other Muslim sects, clearly, disagree with this. The struggle for this change within Islam continues today.

In like manner, Christianity finds itself married to failure on the abortion issue, unless it finds a way to make peace with the modern realities of science. The condemnation of abortion evolved during a pre-industrial era when it's full implications weren't known. It had no scriptural basis, and very little basis in science. Yet during the 1970's and 80's, it was reasoned that opposition to abortion was a winning strategy that Christian leaders could use to gain ground in American politics. Now, that strategy needs to change again. Just as Mormonism rejected polygamy and Islam is (hopefully) in the process of demonizing suicide-terrorism, so Christianity must reject anti-abortionism as a central tenet. As Bishop John Shelby Spong once pointed out (in relation to this as well as many other situations of modern-era ethics) Christianity must change or die.

But for many, it cannot. Because that means letting people make their own choices about sex. Can't have that, can we?

No, *really*. That's what it's all about.

It's about the prospect of allowing citizens to compare a sexually restrictive religion against the sexual freedom science and the secular world provides. With little to offer except blood atonement to go with its sexual buzzkill, a sex-negative religion like Christianity simply has no chance of winning the culture war.

Unless, that is, it can find a wedge issue that forces people to embrace chastity, and consequently fundamentalist Christianity, once again. The abortion issue almost single-handedly transformed the hippies of the Baby Boom generation into some of the most restrictive conservatives America has ever seen. They were tempted by the quick and easy fix of condemning abortion, and for a little while, it seemed to work.

And now, because it has been definitively shown that the brain defines the being, and because the science is not on their side, and even the Bible undermines their position, their gamble is about to come crashing down, dragging Christianity down into minority status along with it.

If only Christian leaders in America could have had the wisdom to have never hitched their wagon to such a falling star.

3. But it's a living thing!

I opened this book with a concession to the pro-life side, and I will now make another one. When the pro-life movement argues that abortion is the taking of human life, they happen to again be absolutely correct. Abortion *is* the snuffing out of something which is both alive, and human. But of course, so is surgery to remove an appendix. For that matter, so is masturbation! Now, I'm not trying to make light of this, at least not in the same sense as Monty Python did in its famous skit they did in the movie *Meaning of Life*, ("every sperm is saaaacred…") but I am trying to make an important point. In the absence of autonomous brain tissue, the remaining bodily tissues simply don't have rights. After all, human cells are cultivated all the time without controversy. *Adult* stem cells are harvested without a second thought from pro-lifers. It is only when an embryo is involved that people get upset. Why? Aren't *non*-embryonic cells also alive and human? Allow me to illustrate:

By now, the reader may be growing tired of "thought experiments," but we shall do just one more. And this time, we'll leave Falwell out if it. In fact, the subject of this experiment will be me. Let's say that I were to take a knife and cut off my left pinky finger. (Not something I'm inclined to do, but in our mind's eye, I'm using plenty of anesthetic.) All of the cells in my severed finger will be alive, and very much human. A few vital signs, such as heartbeat and respiration would be absent, but the cells are living nevertheless. If incubated, they will respire. They have 48 chromosomes, are growing and reproducing (albeit slower these days, since I'm not as young as I used to be), and through cloning, many of them are potential human beings, especially in the bone marrow. In short, they exhibit all of the essential qualities the pro-life movement deems necessary to give those human cells rights. Yet if I fail to reattach my finger, those cells will certainly die. And if I deliberately take my severed finger and cook it in a microwave oven for one minute, those cells will quickly be dead. Have I then committed murder?

Well, of course not! That goes without saying. Severing a finger is doing physical harm, but it is clearly not murder. But notice that in this thought experiment, I *have* taken human life! By cooking my own appendage, I killed that which was alive, human, and even potentially another life. But this comes far short of being genocide. Why?

Part of it has to do with the fact that I only destroyed my own body's parts. This is less genocide and more self-mutilation. It would not be genocide unless I were to kill *all* the cells in my own body at once – and then it wouldn't be genocide, it would be suicide. Yet if someone else had cut off my finger and cooked it, it would still not be murder. More to the point, what would be killed would have no active human brain. Once removed, the nerves in the finger had nothing to communicate their signals to. The cells then "felt" no pain, even as they died by irradiation.

Meanwhile, back in the world where I have ten whole fingers, few on the pro-life side will be satisfied by such rationale. Abortion is indeed the taking of life, and the taking of life is always hard, no matter what the context.

Some may regard all life as sacred, and that this should be honored regardless of whether or not that life can feel pain, or has higher brain function. If so, that is a respectable, if Jainistic[16], objection to abortion. For consistency's sake, such a person should also be a vegetarian. Yet most proponents of abortion are also eaters of red meat, have little objection to war (perhaps in a place like Vietnam, Iraq, Afghanistan or Iran), and are advocates of the death penalty for convicted criminals. Still more oddly, most vegetarians advocate a woman's right to choose. Now we are beginning to get an insight as to why. Liberals are concerned about minimizing suffering in the here and now. Conservatives are more concerned with minimizing suffering in the hereafter.

The bumper-sticker we earlier cited which says, "Abortion stops a beating heart," as we've now seen, puts the emphasis on the wrong organ. Because the brain defines the being, a more apt bumper sticker might read, "Abortion stops a thinking brain." Maybe we could interpret this to mean that the *subject* of abortion causes many people to suspend their own cognitive reasoning processes, and that would certainly be true, but the interpretation we intended, of course, was that abortion might kill a brain which has fully developed. But even *this* would be inaccurate! *Late-term* abortion

---

[16] Jainism is a religion so pacifistic that even the accidental killing of insects is forbidden.

might stop a brain capable of rudimentary thought, but *early term* abortion clearly doesn't. As for beating hearts, butchering livestock for things like pork and hamburger also stops a heartbeat. Yet most pro-lifers typically don't object to having bacon with their eggs during an after-service Sunday Brunch. The process of slaughtering grown pigs inflicts a great deal of pain upon them, yet we as a society do so, mostly without qualm. If a beating heart matters, where is the outrage?

At least with abortion, we spare those among our own species such agony.

4. Basic Instincts

The pro-life persuasion, upon reading this, will undoubtedly seethe with rage at the very notion of these arguments. After all, a fetus is a baby! "Just *look* at it!" they might say. "It's a *baby!*" In more extreme cases, they may hold up poster boards of severed fetal limbs, with the tiny hands clearly visible – an image which evokes a strong emotional response regardless of one's right-wing or left-wing politics. But here is where we must set our maternal and paternal instincts aside, view the scientific evidence with an eye free of colored lenses, and accept the hard facts over our most cherished illusions.

Modern medicine has been able to peer into the womb with cameras and ultrasonic equipment. And it is sometimes crushingly difficult to think of such a visible and moving fetus as anything other than a cherished baby. But we are biologically hard-wired to react this way. To illustrate, consider the following example:

When a little girl has a toy talking-baby-doll, and some mean older brother gruffly shakes it and throws it, the doll subsequently cries (electronically), as does the little girl (actually). Any of us observing this scene would tend to feel sorry, not only for the little girl, *but for the mistreated toy baby, too!* The parents would then harshly scold the older brother for being so mean, telling him he's grounded (and rightly so). But *why* would we feel so sorry for a *toy?* Are we, perhaps like the little girl, just pretending? Or are we *biologically programmed* to feel compassion for something which exhibits baby-like appearance?

I would argue the latter. A fetus at 10 weeks, visibly kicking and punching on the ultrasound monitor, invokes feelings of compassion which often lead us to make a moral judgment. But without a *developed cerebrum*, that growing human fetus, though very much alive and part of the human species, is no more an actual human *being* than the little girl's baby doll!

So a photo of a baby doll's severed limbs has exactly as much meaning as a photo of a 3-month-old fetus' severed limbs, from the standpoint of the brain. (And yes, this is the inspiration of this book's cover image.) It's the *brain*, stupid!

If you think that assessment is a little bit too harsh, you might do well to take a look at the harshness of the situations which arise in a country where the pro-life movement has had its way with government. Ireland is one such country. In the Spring of 2007, a pregnant 17 year-old, whom the press referred to only as 'Miss D,' was prevented from leaving Ireland to have an abortion in England. This, despite the fetus having a rare condition known as *anencephaly*, where most of the brain, part of the scull and scalp were all missing. This unborn baby had no more of a brain than the baby doll we cited earlier. Yet the HSE (Health Service Executive, Ireland's version of Social Services) detained her under law. After a lengthy court battle she was finally allowed to leave. But the case left an indelible mark upon the abortion debate. Even pro-lifers in the United States were silently thanking God they lived in America, and not Ireland! The case of Miss D was, pardon the intentional pun, a complete no-brainer.

For brevity, we'll ignore other such pro-life countries, such as Saudi Arabia, Pakistan or Iran.

One prop I like to use if giving a public talk on the abortion debate is a little plastic replica of a fetus. You often find such replicas handed out at pro life booths at, say, a State Fair, or public event. At one point in my talk, I take the plastic replica and snap its head off. Almost without exception, a number of people in the audience cry out or gasp loudly. I then ask: "Why did you gasp?! It's only plastic!" The reason they gasped, of course, is because of our innate natural programming, which says that if it looks like a baby, it should be protected, brain or not. But in the end, our logic must win out over our emotions.

Of course, it often doesn't. A prototypical example of this comes from the Republican presidential primaries of 2015-2016. During that contentious campaign which saw Donald Trump flabbergast the experts in his rise towards the nomination, there were many also-ran candidates who continued their campaigns for far too long in the common wisdom that people would eventually wise up regarding Trump, and force him out. One of these was former Hewlett-Packard CEO, Carly Fiorina, and she gained notoriety in the race early with her citation of a video showing an aborted fetus, alive and kicking. "I dare Hillary Clinton, Barack Obama to watch these tapes," she said during the second presidential debate on September

16, 2015. Watch a fully formed fetus on the table, it's heart beating, it's legs kicking while someone says we have to keep it alive to harvest its brain." Later, she cited the wrong part of the video, which caused many fact-check organizations to watch the video and conclude that she was lying. But there *was* some video footage which did show what appeared to be a fetus expiring in a stainless-steel bowl, and its appearance movements *are* quite compelling.

Just like any ultrasound of a fetus at 10 weeks would be compelling.

The footage in question was actually of a miscarriage rather than an abortion, but that doesn't really matter. There are many similar videos showing moving fetuses and even moving embryos, and I take Carly Fiorina at her true meaning when she dares liberals to watch such videos and not be moved. One video which I found online was that of a woman's autopsy, and the exposed fetus was visible inside the placenta. One could see its arms and legs distinctly moving on their own, and it was truly hard to watch! But I do not shy away from such images. In fact, I embrace them. I'll not only watch what they want me to see, I will actively show such videos in my talks and on my blog (and already have). Those images make for an emotionally charged argument. But they do not change the fact that the brain defines the being. Arms, legs, and even independent movement do not, as we've seen above.

When you see an exposed fetus, you see hands, fingernails, even a distinctive face. It's very hard to look at that and be dispassionate about there not being someone *in there*. When we humans see a face, even a smiley-face on an emoji, we are programmed to see it as some sort of personality. When cities use an automated radar-device on the side of the highway to tell drivers the speed they are driving and whether they are exceeding the speed limit, studies have shown that drivers slow down far more frequently when the sign also includes a smiling face when the driver isn't speeding, and a frowning face if the driver is going too fast. Why is this? Why do people respond so such simplistic stimuli? After all, the smiling face is nothing more than a sequence of light bulbs which is directed by a computer to make a particular pattern. Yet people respond to the face looking happy or sad depending upon their behavior. It is because we are biologically programmed to ascribe that which looks like a human face, even the caricature of a human face, the attributes of emotional experience – in this case, happy and sad. *This* is how deeply our instincts run when it comes to seeing what looks like a facial pattern. Imagine how deeply that must run when you are seeing the face of a fetus, and not merely a crudely-pixilated smiley.

I remember being a six-year-old child, looking at the corpse of my grandfather at his funeral, lying there in his casket, and feeling that he was still there. I saw no reason why he wouldn't just wake up and ask for his coffee and a newspaper. But he wasn't in there. He was gone. That body was empty. My perception that he was merely asleep was an illusion, given to me by a brain which evolved to see facial patterns and ascribe personalities to them. But there was no "person" in there, anymore.

As hard-heartedly unemotional as it sounds, in a fetus whose brain has not formed past the developmental threshold of basic cognition, there is no person yet either.

5. Stem Cells

Just for the sake of discussion, let's say that a pro-life advocate reading this book is convinced by the brain/being argument, but is somehow not persuaded by the arguments which draw the line at the development of the cerebrum. Let's say he refuses to draw the line at 26 weeks, or even 20 weeks, and insists the line must be drawn further back. He might draw the line at 10 weeks, where the fetus suddenly begins to move and brain stem activity first becomes significant. Then again, he might be even more extreme than this. He might possibly draw the line all the way back at *six* weeks – the earliest point at which *any* kind of brain activity is present at all. He may even push the envelope back to five weeks, just to err on the safe side. If he did, he would have drawn the line at a place which would virtually eliminate the possibility of ever performing an abortion as a means of birth control – by the time the mother discovered her pregnancy, it would already be too late, or very nearly too late. And, upon reading this, I'm certain a large number of pro-lifers will take *exactly* such a position. After all, if the line is drawn at initial brain activity, no matter how remote, and that point is passed by the time the pregnancy is even discovered, then what's the point in defending abortion at all? This position is at least somewhat scientifically respectable in the sense that it obeys what we know about human development and the brain defining the being, though it's a rather extreme interpretation. But would such a pro-life position have any grounds for objection to stem cell research?

The answer is clearly, flatly, and unambiguously, *no!*

Pro-lifers seem to have a presupposed image in their minds that embryonic stem cells are somehow harvested by taking a freshly aborted fetus into some darkened laboratory room, and scraping the cells off of it with a scalpel in some ghastly process that would make even a vivisectionist gag. But this is hardly the case at all. Stem cells are harvested in clean rooms, with micropipettes, laser-tweezers and petri dishes, in a process which never deals with fetal cadavers at all. In fact, it might help to detail exactly how stem cells *are* harvested.

Stem cell harvesting begins by the fertilizing of a human egg in the laboratory. Then, *after only a couple of days*, at the developmental stage in which the growing human cells are referred to as a *blastocyst,* the cells are collected, frozen and stored. This is *almost immediately* after fertilization. The embryo *never* grows to the point of brain development. *Not even close!* For pro-lifers who see reason regarding the brain defining the being, yet still stubbornly oppose abortion on the grounds of protecting life at the first, tiniest spark of any brain-wave activity at all, opposition to stem cell research is simply absurd.

Cases like Tracy Marciniak illustrated the absurdity of drawing the line at the point of birth, and clarified this in the collective mind of the general public, and the media. But stem cell research is the atrocity on the *other* side of the spectrum; the outrage which equally shows how absurd drawing the line at conception is. All over the world, millions – perhaps hundreds of millions – of people suffer from medical maladies which stem cell research holds the promise of curing within their lifetimes, whether it be Alzheimer's disease, paralysis, heart trauma or many, many others.

These myriads of people are literally dying for a cure. They desperately beg for it, and many constantly pray to their God to bring it to them. In the laboratories, God's ministering angels, the scientists, scurry to bring the answer to their prayers. But standing in their way are scientifically ignorant demons to oppose them at every turn, insisting that the cells taken from blastocysts with neither brain nor soul must be protected from the nurturing environment of the Petri dish. They block their funding. They protest their labs. They ignore the pleas of the sick and dying – sacrificing *their* rights, not for the good of the whole, but for the "greater" good of a political ideology. Himmler would be proud.

The old saying holds true, "O, God, please save me from your followers!"

The pro-life movement isn't entirely wrong about there being a holocaust over the abortion issue. Indeed, there is a holocaust. But it is a holocaust of the *born*, not the preborn. Those with Alzheimer's, other forms of dementia, and paralysis are especially anxious for the needed breakthroughs which would give them their lives back. Those with failing organs or degenerative diseases can also have their diseases cured. For some, their only dream is to finally leave the hospital. Even if one stubbornly holds that a few mere cells have rights, what about the rights of these people? What about their families? Must an ocean of tears be shed before their best hope at a medical breakthrough is finally allowed?

And let's also understand that not having every child being loved and wanted is a holocaust too.

With stem cell research, so much more could happen besides. Improved health, improved longevity – perhaps even the ability to live beyond the century mark with sharpness of thought and sprightliness of body! Now, I don't pretend to believe that stem cells hold the promise of immortality. But they might, *just might*, make maintenance of the body as routine as maintenance of a car. A car can run indefinitely – provided that the parts which wear out are continually replaced or repaired. Wouldn't it be amazing to live in a world where all our parts could be replaced – where death wasn't an inevitability that caught up with you after a few short decades! What if stem cells made it possible to live almost indefinitely, to be permanently productive, perhaps even to remain youthful? Ask yourself: what might that be worth to you? Some might kill for it, but if the price were merely the willingness to be open-minded enough to change your position on a controversial issue, would that price seem too high?

6. Rape, and the "Morning After"

One area where the pro-choice side has won victory after victory is in the scenario of what happens if a woman becomes pregnant after being raped. Without exception, the majority of Americans feel that abortion should be available in such cases, and even many who are pro-life hold this view. It offends our sense of justice that a raped woman should have to be saddled with the offspring of the rapist. We desire that the criminal tendency of the raping father not be passed on to the next generation. (Darwinian sexual selection in practice if ever there were a more perfect example!) Yet, if taken to its logical conclusion, the pro-life argument of rights for the unborn would have to be blind to the identities of the parents. A child cannot choose its father, after all. Surely, if the fetus happened to have a rapist father, that's not it's fault! Many, many preachers echo along this same rationale, and more than once I've heard the argument stated thusly: "There are three people involved in a rape scenario: The mother, the baby, and the rapist. So kill the rapist, not the unborn baby!"

I have a certain measure of sympathy for the viewpoint of killing the rapist, even though I happen to be against the death penalty.[17] But deciding whether or not someone dies isn't the only issue. At issue also is whether or not the poor woman gets sentenced to eighteen years hard labor for the mere "crime" of being a victim. If an abortion is not done, she would be given such a sentence, and people know, intrinsically, that this is wrong. Plus, the child would quite possibly not be given the love, care and attention it needed and deserved, given its heritage. Rightly or wrongly, the cycle of criminality would very possibly continue from rapist father to bastard child.

Some argue that there is a genetic component to violence. Current research is still working to determine whether this is true.

---

[17] I acknowledge that there are some crimes which should be punishable by death (terrorists and serial killers) in order to keep our society sane. But our justice system, on occasion, convicts the innocent, or far more frequently, acquits the guilty. I am not comfortable giving a system like that the power to take a person's life. Let it be rare, and on the federal level only.

But if so, then the violent tendencies of the rapist could be passed on to the resultant child, creating a higher curve of societal violence. Stopping this cycle is in all our best interests. True, people tend to frown upon eugenics as Nazi-esque, and rightly so. But why shouldn't we use artificial selection to make us less violent if there is an opportunity to do so ethically?

The case of Miss D (see Chapter 4) is not the only case where Ireland has garnered, well, *ire*, over the abortion issue. In 1992, and later in 2002, teenage girls who had been raped were denied the right to have abortions or travel to England for abortions, after having been raped. Faced with such national embarrassment, Ireland found a loophole: If a rape victim became pregnant, and were subsequently suicidal as a result, then that suicidal tendency would constitute a threat to the life of the mother, and an abortion could be permitted. (!) Thus, a raped girl can get an abortion in Ireland, provided she lies about wanting to kill herself.

Again, in America even some pro-lifers would look at this and silently thank God for Roe v. Wade.

As of yet, this loophole hasn't been used in the United States, but that's only because abortion remains legal. Were abortion to become illegal in the U.S., raped young women would be going suicidal en masse the very next day. Whether they would all be genuine in this claim would be irrelevant. The ability to obtain an abortion would still be theirs. So one wonders, just what does the religious right believe they will accomplish in attempting to take away abortion rights for rape victims? They will not stop abortion. They will merely change its form.

Perhaps the most baffling aspect of rape in relation to abortion is that some pro-lifers actually stand opposed to any sort of "morning after" pill. It's bad enough a woman might be raped. It's even worse that she might become pregnant by such a travesty. It's ten times worse than that to deny this woman an abortion afterward. But to insist that she cannot swallow a pill shortly afterward to make sure than any fertilized ovum never reaches viability? That's not only injustice squared, it's insanity cubed! The pro-life argument has already lost the vote of public opinion when it comes to stem cell research. But the arguments for stem cell research apply with equal force in the case of a raped woman who wants to take a pill the next day or two afterward in order to safeguard the rights of her own body! The only thing being destroyed is a zygote. Any representative of the Church who would deny such a woman the right to do this essentially rapes her a second time.

What about other similar medications, such as RU-486, dubbed by the media as the "French abortion pill?" Well, rape aside, there is really very little objection which can be raised to such a product, given what we've already discussed so far. The argument that the brain defines the being holds up especially well in this context. If a girl misses a period, she takes a pill, crisis averted. Only a few weeks will have gone by, and even those extremists who would draw the line at five or six weeks' development have no defense. Religious pharmacy workers who deny prescriptions for such a drug have to seriously ask themselves just what imaginary moral high ground they think they're standing on.

One final point: If one tactically wanted to maximize the number of abortions possible, the best way to do so would be to deny women the right to any sort of morning after pill. Why? Because any woman who'd already decided to terminate her pregnancy, after being denied such a drug would, of necessity, *have* to receive an abortion later on! The delay in medication merely postpones the inevitable. Every morning after pill denied to a teenager is a virtually guaranteed abortion later! And thus, every pharmacy worker who denies RU-486, or a similar drug is, in effect, a *de facto* abortionist.

Want to minimize or eliminate abortion? Then your best option is to *safeguard* the morning after pill.

7. The Pro-Life Silence About the Brain

It's interesting to note how, when it comes to the brain, those who oppose abortion are often silent. Big signs are made showing the severed portions of aborted fetuses, bumper stickers proclaim that abortion stops a beating heart, and repeatedly the cry of "murder" is heard. But regarding the brain? Very little is said at all.

The website of Missionaries to the Preborn has numerous articles, yet a search of those articles for the keyword "brain" reveals no hits. A similar absence is found in the website of Operation Rescue. Unlike M.T.T.P., the O.R. website has a searchable feature to scan its online articles for keywords. A search for the word "brain" reveals one hit – an article mentioning an abortionist named James McMahon, who died of a *brain* aneurism in 1995 (hence the hit). Pro-Life America has numerous articles searchable by title, with the word "brain" in none of them. The National Right to Life Committee at least links to external articles dealing with fetal brain-related issues, but almost none of them are written by pro-life journals. This author once accompanied a young woman seeking an abortion to a Planned Parenthood clinic in Milwaukee, WI, and thus had the opportunity to read through a pamphlet, made mandatory by law in all abortion clinics in Wisconsin, which described the development of the fetus in some detail – an obvious attempt to make women seeking abortions reconsider. I read through carefully looking for anything at all mentioning the brain, but there was nothing. Randy Alcorn's popular book, *Pro-Life Answers to Pro-Choice Arguments*, mentions brain-wave activity on only three pages, amounting to merely a few short paragraphs – barely a single page (in total) of material dealing with the brain in an annotated volume with over 450 pages! Why is it, that the fulcrum of the entire abortion debate, *the brain*, is scarcely even mentioned in any pro-life literature?

Part of the reason is, that it simply isn't necessary. If the pro-life side is silent about the brain, the pro-choice side is strangely mute about it as well. Both sides are so busy arguing about the fetus as a whole that neither has bothered to deal with the one fetal organ that matters. The consensus seems to be that the human side of the argument must be emphasized, and the complex science of the matter should not be dealt with, since people will simply get lost in the complexity. But I strongly feel that this line of thinking is flat-out wrong. Perhaps I am biased, being a science geek, about educating the public about science. But in our modern-day world, we are bombarded with hyper-complex scientific issues, and the general public needs to be able to deal with them head-on because that's simply the consequence of living in the 21st Century. Not dealing with the complexity of the issue is therefore a severely bad tactical error: we are simply too dependent upon science and technology to grow increasingly ignorant of such subject matter.

Another reason the brain is not more frequently dealt with is because the Supreme Court defined "viability" of a fetus in Roe v. Wade as that which is capable of living outside the mother – something not capable of being done until the fetus' lungs have formed at least to the point where a premature baby can be forced to breathe by artificial means. (Any earlier than about 5 months, and the lungs simply cannot transfer oxygen into the blood.) Yet this definition is arbitrary, and could someday be circumvented with new medical technology. Were it to become possible to transfer a live fetus into an incubating machine and have its umbilical cord "plugged in" to such a device, a fetus could arguably survive outside its mother at nearly any point during a pregnancy – an awe-inspiring possibility which could, if achieved, completely redefine the debate. But the justices of the Supreme Court, while reasonably intelligent, are neither medical doctors nor biologists. Their ruling overlooked the brain, which was, and is, the key factor in anything having to do with fetal development and abortion. As such, those who argued the issue, pro and con, allowed this mistake to define the parameters of the argument.

When the debate shifts to the brain, the pro-choice side tends to win. It really is that simple.

Incidentally, in Randy Alcorn's previously mentioned book, the references to brain development were not only terse, they were misleading. Citing a Newsweek article, it made the argument that a fetus, "early in the second trimester," would attempt to shield its eyes from a probing light with its hand. In fact, that very article ("Do You Hear What I Hear?" Sharon Begley and Tessa Namuth, Special Issue: How Kids Grow, *Newsweek*, June 1, 1991), bluntly stated that the fetus was "mid-term," meaning that it was mid-way through, and

54

not "early in," the second trimester. It also attempted to cite another article claiming that a fetus aged 17 weeks old would begin to engage in REM sleep. While this is essentially true, the book claims (p.77, 2000 edition) that many abortions are still performed at that age, flatly contradicting a pie chart shown several pages earlier (p. 69), showing that fewer than 5% of all abortive procedures are done that late. If one does the math, one finds that 17 weeks is about four months. But 17 weeks is within the 3-4 week variation which comes about from reckoning the onset of a pregnancy at LMP (last menstrual period) versus actual point of conception. So when Randy Alcorn says that REM begins at 17 weeks, he really means 17 weeks from point of conception, but *20 weeks* after last menstrual period, and we already refuted the 20 week threshold in the chapters above.

It is certainly interesting how those few pro-life references which dare to mention the brain end up accidentally supporting the pro-choice side.

8. "Partial-Birth"

So far, we've dealt with winning arguments that deal with the time period at or shortly after conception, since it is during that period of a pregnancy where the pro-choice movement has the most compelling case. But I had also begun this book by conceding the point to the pro-life side regarding the viability of a fetus just prior to birth, and that such a fetus, in fact, has legal rights. I will now backtrack somewhat and argue that even then, the pro-life side does not entirely have a slam-dunk case against the termination of a pregnancy. Oh, they *think* they do, particularly involving the procedure known popularly (or, *un*popularly?) as "partial-birth" abortion. But late-term abortions (as they are more appropriately called) are necessary too, and in many situations are not only ethical, but the most ethical options available.

The reader may been convinced by my arguments thus far (if that is not too presumptuous of me), and perhaps said reader is also convinced as to the need to keep abortion legal during the first two trimesters as a result. But there may be lingering doubts regarding abortion in the third trimester, and that late-term or "partial birth" abortive procedures should therefore be made against the law. Here's just one of many stories involving why that is such a bad idea.

Gretchen Voss was 18 weeks into her pregnancy, and it was time to get an ultrasound to tell if the baby was going to be a boy or a girl. Past the point where miscarriage was an issue, she and her husband Dave were very excited parents-to-be. Dreams about future family life pervaded everything, and they could not have been happier.

But the ultrasound did not go as expected. The technician remained stoic, and Gretchen and Dave could tell that she saw something was wrong. She made some excuse about finishing something on her previous ultrasound, and left the room. The longer she was gone, the more nervous they got. When she finally returned, she directed them to the doctor upstairs. There, they received the terrifying news. The ultrasound had indicated the fetus had an open neural tube defect, meaning that the spinal column had not closed properly, a condition which had a wide variety of possible severities. A trip to another specialist in Boston confirmed the worst. Not only had the spine not closed properly, the location of the neural opening was as bad as it got. The baby would certainly be paralyzed and incontinent. Its brain was being tugged against the opening in the base of the skull and the cranium was full of fluid. The one thing they didn't know was whether the baby would live at all, and if so, with what sort of mental and developmental defects it would have. At the very least, countless surgeries would be required if the baby did live. None of them would repair the damage that was already done.

Knowing that their unborn child faced a short life of suffering and pain, Gretchen and Dave made the hardest decision any parents could make. They decided to terminate the pregnancy.

The procedure was completed on April 7, 2003.

On December 5th later that same year, president George W. Bush signed into law the Partial Birth Abortion Ban Act. Because of a legal challenge, the act didn't go into effect until April 18, 2007, when the Supreme Court ruled on the case of Gonzales v. Carhart. In that case, the court ruled in favor of the law by a 5 to 4 decision.

The law that George W. Bush signed received plenty of fanfare from those on the political right. Only three years before, Bush had won election over Al Gore by the narrowest of margins, and that only because Ralph Nader played spoiler. When the partial birth abortion ban came up to the Supreme Court, Bush had just placed Chief Justice John Roberts onto the bench, stacking the outcome.

It really was *that* close.

"Now, it's like the Stone Age, it's like a Muslim country here," said the doctor who performed Gretchen's procedure. "This is the most backward law, it is not for a civilized country. If this was Iran, Iraq, I wouldn't be surprised. But to pass this law in the United States, what is this government doing?"[18]

What this government is doing is enacting laws governing medicine while being ignorant of the medical realities.

When the "partial birth abortion" procedure is described, it sounds quite brutal. The fetus is pulled out, feet first, while a device is inserted into the skull at the base of the fetus's head. The brain is

---

[18] Boston Globe Magazine, Jan 25, 2004.
http://www.ourbodiesourselves.org/stories/my-late-term-abortion/

sucked out and the skull caved in, making extraction of the fetus much easier. But "partial birth abortion" is not a term recognized by the American Medical Association. It is a term designed to be deliberately incendiary, and to inflame as much passion as possible. Furthermore, the law which made the procedure has become largely irrelevant anyway. If a late-term abortive procedure is to be completed, the preferred practice is now to simply induce fetal demise before removing it. A solution of potassium chloride or digoxin is injected directly into the fetal heart, and thus the fetus is dead before the procedure even begins. Thus, there is no "partial birth" in any legal sense. Only a "partial stillbirth," if that. The much-ballyhooed law enacted under the Bush II administration was easily circumvented.

But this is a good thing. People are biologically very diverse, and their medical needs vary greatly from patient to patient. Sometimes this results in a horrible choice between two evils, and no one wants a medically ignorant legislator dictating terms in such a situation.

As another example of this, take Dana Weinstein. After receiving a sonogram at 29 weeks into her pregnancy, she learned that her unborn daughter's brain hadn't formed properly. Only a few weeks before, she had learned that George Tiller had been gunned down in his church by an anti-abortion extremist. She sat there rubbing her third-trimester belly thinking, 'I don't know how anybody this late in the pregnancy could have an abortion.' She had always been for the right to choose, but didn't understand why someone would have a late-term abortion. But there, as her sonogram procedure was done a few weeks later, Weinstein understood exactly why. The sonogram detected abnormalities. The technician noted that the ventricles in the baby's brain were enlarged and that the fetus seemed to be having difficulty swallowing. It was June 26, 2009.

An MRI several weeks later confirmed that the baby, dubbed "Baby W," suffered from multiple malformations of the brain. The connections between the right and left brain had not formed, a condition called agenesis of the corpus callosum. The baby also had polymicrogyria, a severe brain condition where the ridges don't form properly, which can cause intellectual and physical disabilities, as well as seizures that are "difficult or impossible to control with medication," according to the National Institutes of Health.

"We noted a number of different brain malformations," explained Rhonda L. Schonberg, the coordinator at the Center for Prenatal Evaluation at Children's National Medical Center in Washington, DC, where Weinstein was given the diagnosis. "Her fetus was really at a significant risk for developmental delay and seizure disorder." It was a rare diagnosis, and it's unclear what caused it, Schonberg said. It was also a condition that was not clear in Weinstein's 20-week checkup, because most brain development occurs in the third trimester, so it would have been difficult to foresee this earlier in the pregnancy.

Weinstein was faced with the prospect of giving birth to a baby that was expected to suffer from nearly constant seizures, could have required feeding tubes to stay alive, and could have been in a vegetative state, if it survived at all. She decided to end the pregnancy rather than continuing for another two months and prolonging the suffering. It was a very personal decision, she says, one made between her, her family, and her doctors. "We wanted her and loved her," Weinstein says. "In some ways I feel a little bit lucky, in that she was so sick that the decision was almost made for us. I don't wrestle with guilt."

Even though she lived in Maryland and saw a doctor in Washington, DC, Weinstein found it difficult to obtain an abortion so far along in her pregnancy. There were no doctors, at the time, that offered the procedure at her stage in the Washington area. She had to travel to Dr. Warren Hern's clinic in Boulder, Colorado, far from her support network. Weinstein spent a week in Colorado between the initial visit with the doctor and the actual procedure, all the time worrying that the baby was suffering. It wasn't until July 14 that she was able to undergo the procedure. "I don't have words to describe the agony of those days," she says. But, "knowing how sick the child was, I can't imagine ever being forced to carry the baby to term."

The ordeal was expensive. The Weinsteins racked up $17,500 in medical bills, and it took a lengthy fight with their insurance company to get the procedure covered. There was also airfare and the hotel stay to cover. But as hard as that was, if there had been a 20-week abortion ban been the national law, she would

60

not have been able to have had the procedure at all. The baby would have to have been carried to term, removed by caesarian section, then kept on incubators until it died shortly after birth at great expense to everyone.

That anti-abortion groups have premised their 20-week bans in a number of states on "fetal pain" ignores the fact, Weinstein says, that in her case she sought to end the suffering of her baby. "I'm not going to be made to feel ashamed because I allowed her to have a peaceful death," she says.

And therein lies the ultimate irony. In attempting to safeguard a fetus on the grounds that it can feel pain after 20 weeks, "Baby W" would have ended up suffering horrifically, and needlessly.

Abortions like Weinstein's are quite rare. Only 1.4 percent of all procedures occur at 21 weeks or beyond, according to the Centers for Disease Control. Most of those procedures happen because a life-threatening medical problem or a fetal abnormality only became apparent at a later date. But even in Washington, DC, there are few options for women in Dana's situation who seek an abortion.[19]

If a doctor is not given every tool at his disposal to be able to make the best possible medical decision for his patients, then he is put into a terrible position where he cannot adequately give care, even though the technology is present. Worse, he may have to choose between proper care for his patient, or breaking the law – something no doctor should ever have to face in a civilized society.

Consider yet another example in Tiffany Campbell. When she was 19 weeks pregnant, Tiffany and her husband Chris learned her pregnancy was afflicted with a severe case of twin-to-twin transfusion syndrome, a condition where the two fetuses unequally share blood circulation. The diagnosis was that one of the fetuses had a strained heart and acute risk of heart failure while the other had a blood supply that was insufficient to sustain normal development. The Campbells were told that without a selective termination, they risked the loss of both. At 22 weeks, in consultation with their doctors, they made the difficult decision to abort one fetus in order to save the other.[20]

---

[19] http://www.motherjones.com/politics/2011/07/late-term-abortion-29-weeks-dana-weinstein

Had a 20-week abortion ban been enacted in that state, the doctors would have had no choice but to watch *both* fetuses die, because they wouldn't be able to terminate either one! I ask you, is that very smart legislation?

The phrase "partial birth" itself was always a misnomer, deliberately word-smithed to be as incendiary as possible. The gory details of what a physician has to do in order to perform the "partial birth" abortive procedure are well known, and indeed, it seems difficult to justify its practice in light of this. But they are irrelevant, and not just because medical science has ways around it. In the rare cases that a late-term abortion *has* to be done, the fetus is almost assuredly doomed anyway, and the brain has almost never past the point of viability. If the required length of time has somehow passed, the brain is often not viable anyway, as the deformities often affect the brain in the most serious of cases. In short, as gory as a "partial birth" procedure may be, it pales in comparison to the kind of malady the fetus has already been stricken with.

Take the case of Vikki Stella, a diabetic, who discovered months into her pregnancy that the fetus she was carrying suffered from several major anomalies and had no chance of survival. Because of Vikki's diabetes, her doctor determined that induced labor and Caesarian section were both riskier procedures for Vikki than an abortion. The procedure not only protected Vikki from immediate medical risks, but also ensured that she would be able to have children in the future.[21] In cases like Vikki's, the doctor and patient were both lucky enough to have the legal option to do the right thing for Vikki's health, unencumbered by legislators chasing imaginary dragons to slay. But other women aren't so fortunate.

Danielle Deaver was 22 weeks pregnant when her water broke. Tests showed that Danielle had suffered anhydramnios, a premature rupture of the membranes before the fetus has achieved viability. Without sufficient amniotic fluid, the fetus likely would be born with a

---

[20] Public Hearing on LB1103 before the Committee on Judiciary, Nebraska Legislature, (Neb. 2010) (testimony of Tiffany Campbell).
[21] Partial Birth Abortion Ban of 1995: Hearing on H.R.1833/S. 939 before the Senate Comm. on the Judiciary,
104th Cong. (1995) (testimony of Vikki Stella).

shortening of muscle tissue that results in the inability to move limbs. In addition, the fetus likely would suffer deformities to the face and head, and the lungs were unlikely to develop beyond the 22-week point. The couple, in counsel with their doctor, explored every possible action to save the pregnancy. However, there was less than a 10-percent chance that, if born, the baby would be able to breathe on its own and only a two-percent chance the baby would be able to eat on its own. They decided to terminate the pregnancy and asked the doctor if she could help them "put an end to this nightmare." The doctor's response... "no, [I] can't." Under the Nebraska ban, which had been in effect for just two months, the Deavers had no recourse to avert the pain and suffering that was to follow. Eight days later, after Danielle endured intense pain and infection, their daughter Elizabeth was born and survived for just 15 minutes.[22] Once again, good-hearted but misled politicians ended up doing more harm than good, inflicting deliberate pain on the innocent for the sake of the already doomed.

A pregnancy which threatens a woman's life late-term can usually be dealt with by caesarian section, and a fetus after 23 weeks is capable of surviving outside the mother as a "preemie," making the partial-birth abortion debate somewhat moot. Yet the rare occurrence does take place, and medicine is fraught with tales of the unexpected crisis. The case of Gianna Molla would likely be dealt with easily with today's medical technology, but for a woman carrying a fetus with severe hydrocephalitis (essentially, "water on the brain"), the prospect of a normal birth can be virtually nil. Dr. William F. Henderson once wrote, "It is not unusual for the fetal head to be as large as 50 centimeters [about 20 inches] in diameter and may contain... close to 2 gallons of cerebrospinal fluid."[23] In such cases as these, options are limited, and the fetus is already doomed. (Interestingly, with all the brave talk about making exceptions for the health or life of the mother, no one talks about what should happen in those cases where the health/life of the *fetus* is moot.) There are only two options: caesarian section, or *D&C*

[22] Jason Clayworth, Her Baby Wasn't Expected to Live, But Nebraska Law Banned Abortion, DES MOINES REGISTER, Mar. 6, 2011.

[23] http://www.gentlebirth.org/archives/hydrceph.html

(dilation and curettage), sometimes referred to as D&X (dilation and extraction), the medical term for the "partial-birth abortion" procedure.

One can easily imagine what could happen if legislators took to heart the wild-eyed opinion of former Surgeon General C. Everett Coop (who once said that no competent physician ever needs to perform a D&C) and all such procedures were then made illegal. The only option for the poor pregnant woman in the above example would then be a caesarian, thus greatly increasing her chances for infection, jeopardizing her chances for having children in the future, and exposing her to potential life-threatening surgical trauma. That's hardly fair. Because of situations like the above, nearly all legislation designed to make D&C procedures illegal include a clause which would make an exception in cases to protect the mother. But conservative interests want to all but stop the procedure altogether, and so that exception is deemed necessary, in their legislative wording, only when the *life* of the mother is at risk. Opponents to such legislation object because they feel that such phrasing is too restrictive, and that the exception should include situations to protect the *health* of the mother. In the above example, after all, the decision to perform a D&C instead of a caesarian is not a life/death decision, but one designed to protect the mother's overall well-being. It is then counter-argued that "health" could mean anything, and that such an exception would render the procedure functionally legal again. In light of D&C being rarely performed anyway, this seems like paranoia—and it is. Thus it seems the best possible way to resolve the issue is not to ban D&C procedures, but rather to accord a late-term fetus legal rights. Currently, our nation's laws already do this.

In 1996, the American College of Obstetrics and Gynecologists thoroughly reviewed D&C procedures, and determined that there were no circumstances where "partial-birth abortion" was the only option to save the life or preserve the health of a pregnant woman. But they did find that there *were* a number of circumstances where it would be the *best course of action* out of all available options, and recommended that only a doctor, in consultation with the patient, should make such a decision.[24]

---

[24] "*Statement on So-Called "Partial Birth Abortion*" Laws By The American College of Obstetricians and Gynecologists," 2002-FEB-13, at:

Translation: The *medical professionals and the patients* should be the ones making the medical decisions instead of special-interest legislators in Washington, almost none of whom have a medical degree.

Yet in spite of the ACOG's opinion, I would strongly argue that there are situations where an abortion *is* the only way to save the life of a woman. Dr. George Tiller, for example, once performed an abortion for a woman from Palestine whose ultra-conservative Muslim family would certainly have killed her had her late-term pregnancy been discovered.[25] In this case, Tiller's procedure quite literally saved her life. The ACOG only considered medical reasons that might threaten the life of the mother, but there are non-medical reasons that might threaten the life of the mother as well, and they needn't be Muslim or even religious in nature. A viciously vindictive father or jealous sociopathic boyfriend is hardly out of the question, even in the secular world, and either one could realistically kill a woman with a baby fathered by someone the father or boyfriend disapproves of.

Tiller saved the lives of many other women whose *wanted* pregnancies (in some cases *desperately* wanted) were forced to be terminated due to a mother's life-threatening condition, or because the fetus had some horrific heart-breaking defect. Tiller, being one of the few men in the nation who was both willing and qualified to perform late-term abortions, literally saved hundreds of lives.

On May 31, 2009, while serving as an usher inside his Lutheran church, George Tiller received a lifetime achievement award from Mr. Scott Roeder – in the form of a bullet to the head.

We've seen some real-life stories, but now imagine the following hypothetical scenario. (Not quite a "thought experiment." More of a "what if" prediction.) A pregnant woman, we'll call her Mary Moe, has her fetus diagnosed with hydroencephalitis, and it's a severe case. She'd gone for regular checkups, but the ultrasound discovered the problem late, through no fault of her own. She's

---

http://www.acog.org/from_home/publications/press_releases/nr02-13-02.cfm

[25] This according to Annie Laurie Gaylor, as voiced on Freethought Radio, June 6, 2009. Why such barbaric travesties as Sharia-based "honor killings" should persist into the 21st century is an issue left for a separate volume.

horrified and saddened to know her baby will die, and struggles to come to terms with it. But first, the fetus must be extracted. The safest means of doing so would be a D&C, but there's a problem. A conservative administration was recently elected, and a complete ban on partial birth abortion was passed into law, with no exception for a mother's health – only her life. The doctor has no choice but to perform a caesarian. The patient is put under, her belly cut open, and the fetus with its swollen and distended head is removed. A shunt is inserted into the skull of the baby in a last-ditch hope-against-hope effort to save it, but it inevitably dies a short while later anyway. But the mother has not reacted well to the anesthetics, and her blood is clotting poorly. After surgery, she is given a small amount of a clotting drug to help her body heal its internal wounds. But this results in an unforeseen consequence. A blood clot develops in her meningeal artery, which later migrates to her brain. She suffers a massive stroke. In spite of all the hospital's efforts to treat her, she develops complications, contracts pneumonia, and dies two weeks later.

This scenario, though imaginary, is not at all unlikely, should conservatives who wish to ban all partial birth abortions have their way. And it's only one of hundreds of possible ways a woman could die if a physician is forced to needlessly slice her belly open. Picture for a moment how quickly such a story would spread throughout the liberal media. Imagine how outraged the general public would be. "Mary Moe" would become an icon of the culture wars, and an even bigger name than Terry Schaivo, or "Baby M." "Mary should not have died!" Activists would protest. "The conservatives killed her!" In short order, a bill would be drafted to reverse the ban on partial birth abortion. It would likely be vetoed by the conservative president, who would subsequently lose his bid for reelection. Much more would die than simply this woman. Arguably, conservatism as a popular movement would die with her. Oh, it would resurface again in a different form, to be sure; lower taxes and old-fashioned values will always find a foothold somewhere, somehow. But the religious would be forever shut out from its decision-making. After all, it could never afford to allow another failure like "Mary Moe."[26]

---

[26] I've been asked, "What if medical advancements make it possible to rescue a fetus with severe hydroencephaly, or other such maladies which would make a

66

To those on the pro-life side, I would ask, is *this* the future you want?

D&C the best option? Wouldn't that shift the debate?" My answer to this is, yes it would. Ironically, the only thing which could achieve these medical breakthroughs is stem cell research!

9. Conclusion

Let's consider what the world would be like if abortion were banned in the United States. We don't have to use our imagination. All we have to do is look back in recent history. An entire generation of young people don't know what it was like living in a world where "coat hanger abortions" were a reality, but a marvelous documentary called "The Coat Hanger Project" has kept the memory alive. Prior to Roe v. Wade, desperate young women turned to gouging a crude wire up into their cervixes in an attempt to self-abort. Many of these young women died.

Here's just one story from those dark pre-Roe times.

In the fall of 1969, four years before Roe v. Wade, a Milwaukee physician named Sydney Babbitz was arrested and charged with the crime of performing abortions in his office. The penalty was up to fifteen years in prison, and the loss of his medical license. His lawyers took the case all the way to Federal court, and by January of 1970, the case was heard. A three-judge panel comprised of former Wisconsin governor John Reynolds, former Illinois governor Otto Kerner, and Myron Gordon, heard arguments from both sides.

In March of 1970, the panel handed down its verdict. By a unanimous decision, they ruled Wisconsin's anti-abortion law was unconstitutional.

With the law struck down, some brave souls in Madison, Wisconsin, among them Dr. Alfred Kennan and Anne Nicol Gaylor, decided to open the first abortion clinic. They were flooded with calls months in advance and had to refer hundreds of women to a clinic in Mexico City, Mexico. The clinic, called the Midwest Medical Center, finally opened in February of 1971, the first and only clinic of its kind from East Coast to West Coast. It helped hundreds of women from all over the nation and was booked for weeks in advance.

Then, on April 19, 1971, Madison police shut down the clinic in a Gestapo-like raid. Keep in mind, according to the Federal court ruling, the clinic was legal, and the raid was illegal, but that didn't stop police from raiding the clinic anyway. The clinic workers were arrested, expensive equipment was seized, and Anne Nicol and Dr.

Kennan were subjected to hours of pointless questions to which they pleaded the fifth amendment.

After months of legal dispute and thousands of taxpayers' dollars wasted, the clinic finally reopened on May 24, 1971, but the damage had been done. Many women arrived at the clinic after days of travel, only to find the doors locked without explanation. The patients could not be contacted regarding the shutdown – the appointment book had been seized during the raid.

Sadly, this cost one young woman her life, as Anne Nicol Gaylor recounted in her book, 'Abortion is a Blessing.' This unnamed girl and her boyfriend had an appointment the week the clinic was shut down, and found the doors locked on them. They were understandably afraid, and didn't know where else to turn. The boyfriend made several tentative phone calls to various medical outlets, but was rebuffed at every turn, told how expensive the procedure could be, how there could be legal consequences, parental counseling needed, etc. etc. Unsure of what else they could do, the young woman finally took matters into her own hands. Not telling her boyfriend, she took a coat hanger and jabbed it into her uterus. Later, when her physical pain became too much to bear, she finally confessed what she'd done to her boyfriend. He panicked, not knowing where to turn. He finally phoned collect to a clergyman he felt he could trust. That minister assured him that his fears of legal retribution were overblown and that he needed take his girlfriend to a hospital right away. He even offered to help. Relieved, he got his girlfriend to the hospital. But they were too late. The coat hanger had perforated her uterine wall badly, and she bled internally to death a few hours after arriving at the emergency room.

Approximately 600 women were turned away during the period in which the Midwest Medical Center was shut down (about 120 women per week multiplied by five weeks). According to the Guttenmacher Institute, 1.06 million abortions were performed in 2011 alone.[27] The 1971 Madison shutdown resulted in at least one death per 600 patients. If we take the Guttenmacher figure of 1 million abortions performed and turn that into 1 million denied, then divide that figure by 1 death per 600 denied abortions, we get nearly 1,700 dead by coat hanger abortion, and this is quite a low estimate

[27] https://www.guttmacher.org/fact-sheet/induced-abortion-united-states

given how many abortions are already being denied. This gives us just a small glimpse of just how horrifying it would be to live in America, if anti-abortionists got their way.

Another consequence might be what happens during an ectopic pregnancy. An ectopic pregnancy happens when the fertilized egg attaches itself, not to the uterine wall, but to the inside of one of the fallopian tubes[28]. This is not life threatening to the mother – at first. But if not aborted immediately, the pregnancy becomes very life-threatening indeed! Severe internal bleeding and the inability to conceive again are just some of the potential consequences of not performing an abortion immediately in such cases. But if anti-abortion laws only protect cases where the life of the mother is in crisis rather than the health of the mother, then such pregnancies must be put off, until it is too late, and doctors are forced to violate their Hippocratic Oaths under penalty of law.

Yet another consequence of abortion being outlawed would be an increase in crime. In their marvelous book *Freakanomics* (2005), Steven Levitt and Steven Dubner dealt with how abortion affects the crime rate. They began with pointing out how crime increased in Romania in the mid-80's, stemming from Nicolae Ceaușescu's policy of strictly outlawing abortions. They then cited the way that crime in America so precipitously dropped in the early 1990's. What could have caused crime to drop so drastically? The one sure-fire predictor of criminality, they pointed out, was/is being male between the ages of 18 and 25. It might not have been politically correct to say so, but Levitt and Dubner did. Thus it follows that if there were more males in that age range who were economically destitute in a given era, crime would be higher during that era. In other words, the number of males between 18 and 25 who were in poverty drastically went down in the early 90's. The cause? Levitt and Dubner point to the only explanation that made any sense: That in 1973, abortion became legal. More male babies born after that time were wanted rather than unwanted. The number of unwanted pregnancies that resulted in a male births went drastically down. 18 to 20 years later, crime rates fell through the floor.

---

[28] https://www.womenonweb.org/en/page/525/what-is-an-ectopic-pregnancy-and-how-do-you-know-you-have-one

Naturally, there were many who hated this conclusion! One author named John R. Lott, Jr., even wrote an entire book called *Freedomnomics*, ostensibly to debunk that one point alone. However, upon reading the book, the bulk of it turns out to be dedicated to unrelated topics like supply-side economics and gun control. Only near the very end of the book does the subject of Levitt and Dubner's assessment of crime even get discussed, and *that* only as barely a blurb amongst an argument largely centered on the belief that an increase in concealed gun-carry laws was responsible for the decrease in crime during the early 90's. He then goes on to argue that an increase in restrictive gun laws seems to have no measurable effect upon crime rates. In other words, *decreasing* gun restrictions makes crime go down, but *increasing* gun restrictions does not affect crime either way! It's a classic case of wanting to have it both ways.

Most pro-life arguments against the model proposed by *Freakanomics* are equally inept. The link between abortion bans and high crime roughly two decades later is a very real one! And that means that banning abortion will mean, for the generation of children born on or after that fateful day, living in a world less safe, less secure, with higher crime. This in turn will drive down jobs as employers seeking stable regions in which to do business will go elsewhere, and even more crime will result. What a horrible thing to do to the next generation!

Now let's examine what the world would be like where it were universally recognized that the brain defines the being; a world where the third trimester is the line of quickening – drawn at neither conception nor birth, and it is possible to be both pro-life *and* pro-choice. Gianna Molla would likely have been able to receive an ethical abortion using this standard, and live to have and care for her children, and perhaps many more. Tracy Marciniak would be able to sue for manslaughter (and win) because her late-term fetus clearly had legal rights. Young teenage girls would never have to be saddled with an overwhelmingly crushing burden just because they were either attacked by a rapist, or just plain young enough to err in their ways – something we've all done. Every girl would have legal power over her own body, and every expectant mother would have in-utero protection under the law. No woman would have to endure having their insurer refuse coverage for contraceptive care. It certainly sounds an awful lot better than the kind of mess we have now! I suggest we make it a reality.

I'm not so naïve as to think this actually settles the issue. Far from it! The famous astronomer, Dr. Carl Sagan, and his wife, Ann Druyan, two people far wiser than myself, attempted to voice a similar opinion to the one I've outlined here in the April 22, 1990 issue of Parade magazine. They discovered, to their horror, that almost *nobody* approved of it. I expect little better when the notion merely comes from my lowly self. The fighting will continue. Doubtless some will read this and find my ramblings to be nothing short of an academic's philosophizing of a national holocaust. Others might read this and be genuinely convinced. Yet it is quite obvious that, regardless of one's persuasion, the pro-choice side tends to win arguments pertaining to the early term of a pregnancy, and the pro-life side tends to win in the late term of a pregnancy. In the end, this particular tug of war will inevitably end in a tie, just as it always has. The midway point (26 weeks) will eventually win out as the standard. Perhaps not in this generation, but someday. In the meantime, both sides remain entrenched, inflexible, and closed-minded for the long-term.

The premise of this book hangs on the notion of what science has taught us about the brain, and fetal development. It might then be countered, if science is so clear about the implications in the abortion debate, why aren't more scientists, outside of stem-cell researchers, speaking up in favor of abortion? The answer has to do with funding. As with so many things, if you want to know why things are done a certain way, follow the money. Scientists typically receive their paychecks either from an academic institution or through some funding arm of the government. Only on more rare occasions is there a private grant which allows them to work. Naturally, speaking out on controversial issues is exactly the sort of thing which can make institutions and politicians nervous, which in turn jeopardizes funding. Even private donors can become nervous if what they fund receives too much bad publicity. As such, scientists choose their battles carefully. They leave the abortion debate to others, and try to quietly go about their research. Perhaps someday the paradigm will shift, and some institutions will be less fearful of potential consequences in giving the scientific consensus. But until then, the silence of professional scientists regarding this issue should not surprise us.

Also not dealt with here was the semi-related subject of euthanasia. Many pro-lifers cite it as a means of garnering consistency on the point of sanctity of life, since many pro-choice advocates also support the elderly's right to die. The sad case of Teri Schiavo, whose persistent vegetative state triggered a much publicized series of lawsuits culminating in the removal of her feeding tube in 2005, has often been cited by pro-life groups as a consequence of pro-choice thinking. But abortion deals with the beginning of a life, and euthanasia deals with a mature adult's decision to end it. This book simply does not deal with that end of the timeline. For the record, however, this author supports the idea of the living will – if someone of clear and sound mind legally notes that they never wish to be preserved in a vegetative, comatose, or even severely mentally damaged state, then we must respect that person's end-of-life decision. Teri Schiavo should have drawn up such a document before her tragic illness.

This book has the makings of a late-blooming success, because at some point in the not-too-distant future, the human population will finally hit its maximum ceiling. There are over 7 billion people on planet Earth at the time of this writing (2015). That figure will reach 9 billion as early as 2030. Sooner or later, there will be too many mouths to feed and not enough food to go around. We already have this condition in some parts of the world, but do not generally feel its effects here in the Western Democracies because our wealth protects us from it. Yet the starvation in foreign lands is very real and cannot be denied! It surfaces regularly when we are watching television in the middle of the night, and some white-bearded man or washed up celebrity pops up in a commercial to prick our conscience and ask for funds to "feed the children." (The adults, I often muse, can apparently rot in hell.) With people in China eating such delicacies as scorpions-on-a-stick, and Latin Americans going north of the Mexican/U.S. border *en masse* just to find their next meal, how long will it be before that starvation creeps up noticeably within your local grocery store? Estimates may vary on just exactly how many humans our planet can sustain before the middle-classes of the more wealthy nations begin to starve for lack of food, but we are almost certainly already close to this point now, and the only reason we have not yet reached it is because our scientists (in particular, agricultural scientist Dr. Norman Borlaug) have literally saved our lives by giving us genetically modified plants which can produce more food per acre, and in harsher climates. And yet despite this success, anywhere from one third to one half of our cereal grains are wasted as cattle-feed to sustain our excessively large craving for meat. This will become quite unsustainable in the mid-21st Century! To have enough to feed everyone, meat will have to be largely replaced with other plant-based products. And all this still leaves out the looming threats to our ability to even grow and sustain the crops of tomorrow. Global climate change threatens to destabilize and drastically reduce the number of acres we can effectively farm. Disappearing ice caps and melting glaciers threaten to eliminate the worldwide fresh water supplies upon which every farmer dearly depends. Desperate fishermen will be sorely tempted to over-harvest our oceans, not realizing that they are destroying tomorrow to feed today. Meanwhile, well-meaning yet naïve young people protest "Frankenfoods," not fathoming how they are undermining the hybrid crops we will so desperately need to rely upon both for today and tomorrow. Eventually, to ensure the world's economies, and to avoid global starvation, the nations of the planet will have no choice but to unite in enacting across-the-board population controls. Many will object, but the growling of hungry stomachs will ensure the universal approval of voters. Birth control will, inevitably, be mandated.

In short, today's abortion debate is but a minor skirmish. The *real* war is yet to come! Guess which side will lose?

Most of us know a story or two involving an investor who put all his savings into one, big investment, and then went bankrupt after that investment bottomed out. Conservative Christianity seems to be just such a foolish spender, having put in much time, energy, and so very, very much money into defeating abortion. So much has been spent in their fight. So very much has been wasted. Nearly all of the time they have done this, the people involved in this effort felt they were doing the will of God. All that time, they were wrong. If there is a will of God on this issue at all, it seems to me that it would be doing the maximum to achieve the highest quality of life for all. Inflicting wide-spread suffering upon grown teenagers and adults for the sake of growing human cells not yet conscious of pain seems the exact *opposite* of what any God would want – to say nothing of being a violation of every principle of common sense. Certainly, a loving God would wish us to respect the sanctity of life. But one can certainly respect life's sanctity without being handcuffed by it. We *must* destroy life to live, whether it is eating a chicken sandwich or merely crunching a fruit with our teeth. Let us therefore respect the sacrifice of that life as part of Divine Providence, and make sure that when we must destroy living human cells, we always do so ethically.

Afterword: Literally Saving America

There are lots of "wedge issues" in politics. There's gun rights, for example, or the legalization of marijuana, or gay rights, global warming, evolution in public schools, prayer in public schools, trickle-down economics, or instituting the death penalty. But the biggest one since the late 70's has been abortion. If there's one issue that has forced otherwise sensible people to vote for one candidate over another, it's that one. How did this happen?

The landmark Supreme Court decision of Roe v. Wade took place in 1973. This became a wake-up call among many Christian clergymen and they felt they needed to do something. At the same time, Republican leaders realized that, after decades of winning over white racist voters in the South, white favoritism was a dying cause, and Cold War rhetoric wasn't going over very well with an electorate which was waking up to the fact that nuclear war was tantamount to suicide. They needed a new issue, one which would help bolster their numbers. Eventually, they sided with religious leaders on the issue of abortion, and it was one hell of a watershed decision!

Frank Schaeffer, the son of evangelist Francis Schaeffer, worked with his father and other Christian leaders such as Jerry Falwell, Pat Robertson and James Dobson to establish the Moral Majority. Frank details the story in his book, *Crazy For God*, and I highly recommend it. Up until this point in history, abortion was only something Catholics cared anything about. Evangelicals had fully embraced contraception and all its benefits. What changed?

What changed was how the public saw abortion. In response to a huge PR campaign to demonize abortion as a modern-day holocaust, the tide of public opinion began to turn. So successful was this ad blitz that it literally halted the sexual revolution in its tracks. Over the course of a decade, the Baby Boomer generation that reveled in the Summer of Love in 1968, celebrated free love at Woodstock, and challenged religious assumptions at every turn became the generation that became so rabidly conservative that the very word "liberal" became a dirty word to many. By the time the AIDS scare of the 1990's was taking place, the sexual revolution was over – strangled by a condom and drowned out by chants of "safe sex" and "abstinence is the only sure protection."

Jimmy Carter was the first president elected after Roe v. Wade in 1976, largely on him being a Southern Baptist Christian. In a debate among other democratic party candidates, when they were all asked wo their role models were, most gave answers like, "Thomas Jefferson" or "Abraham Lincoln." Then Carter, smiling broadly, answered, "The role model in my life is Jesus Christ." And all the other Democratic candidates knew they'd lost their election bid at that point. Carter easily defeated Gerald Ford, who had been rightly demonized for pardoning Richard Nixon.

But that momentum shifted when Carter sided with women's rights and backed Planned Parenthood. Overnight he was demonized by the religious right and lost the Christian vote. This helped Reagan win election in 1980. Reagan then sided with the pro-life side. One of his last acts in office was to remove the Fairness Doctrine from the list of FCC regulations. The Fairness Doctrine required broadcasters to present both sides of any controversial issue. With its removal, broadcasters could now preach only one side of a political debate and never have to deal with counter-arguments. What could persuade a fair-minded guy like Reagan to do something so contrary to free speech? Abortion.

In 1996, Bill Clinton signed the Telecommunications Act into law, deregulating the airwaves across the United States. This lifted the cap on the number of broadcasting stations a company could own, and the result was one company, Clear Channel, dominating the radio market, and putting only conservative talk show hosts on the air. What could persuade media moguls like Rupert Murdoch and Roger Ailes to amass such a vast propaganda machine in this way? Again, abortion.

As I write this chapter, Donald Trump has just been elected president, winning the electoral college while losing the popular vote – with the largest disparity between the two in history. While there were many factors which contributed to this travesty, the fact that Donald Trump presented himself as the pro-life candidate was one major reason it happened. In the third and final televised debate between himself and Hillary Clinton, he gave a rant about partial-birth abortion which was truly one for the extremist record books. Hillary Clinton, by contrast, gave a sensible and level-headed statement in which she stood by women's reproductive rights. What could have persuaded so many people to vote for such a disqualified (yes, I said *dis*qualified) candidate? Abortion, again. But at least we now have a weapon to fight back, at least regarding the subject of abortion. The anti-abortion movement started this downfall, and I think defeating it could reverse the trend.

"The brain defines the being." Five words! And they have been undefeated in debate every time they have been used. Part of why I put this forth in this book is because, maddeningly, nobody else is stepping up to the microphone and saying this. But it's the inoculation that will destroy the virus. It's high time we used it.

No, this is not a magic bullet which will save America in four years. It will not win the Culture War overnight. But it *will* win the Culture War! And that means that America can be saved. Liberalism has gained major strides in recent decades and has defeated conservatism on every front – except one; women's rights. Why? Again, opposition to abortion. Clear the field of that, and you pave the way for sensible legislation in politics as moderates return to Capitol Hill.

It's an uphill battle, and it will take many years, but we have the winning argument, and that gives us the upper hand. "The brain defines the being" is a devastatingly effective phrase. Let's use it!

Appendix

The Trial of Avery Froelich
By Eric J. Hildeman
(Originally published in Bastion Science Fiction Magazine, April 2014.)

Even the inept policemen on Mars Colony Six could tell that the old man, Tyrell Horopecci, had been murdered. Officially, no crime ever took place in Sixth Colony, or so said the brochures. Unofficially, well, the multiple gunshot wounds would have made the situation obvious enough, even if the body weren't missing a head, which it was.

The obvious suspect was his son-in-law, Avery Froelich, who stood to inherit the entire estate. Police had actually once suspected him of foul play before when his wife, Horopecci's daughter, conveniently disappeared. This time, however, Froelich had no alibi, and police were able to make an arrest. Now, with the murder trial finally underway, it seemed as though prosecutors were about to blow their case like a Martian dust storm. However, the lead prosecutor had a remarkable trump card up his sleeve and was about to play it.

"Continuation of The People vs. Avery Simon Froelich. Charge of murder in the first degree. Court is now in session," announced the bailiff.

"Very well," replied the presiding Honorable Judge Morris, banging his gavel. He was dressed in his Martian-red robes rather than the more traditional black robes worn on Earth, with the similarly traditional faux bald head instead of a powdered wig. Such bald-caps were worn in honor of the early Martian pioneers who had lost their hair due to exposure to cosmic rays. On Mars, bald was not only beautiful, it was powerful, too.

"Your Honor," announced a similarly bald-capped Fredrick Stroh, District Attorney, "if there are no objections, I would like to call our final witness to the stand."

81

"Mr. Burgbe, any objections?" asked the judge.

"Your Honor, I don't recall that the prosecution *has* any witnesses left to call upon," answered Romney Burgbe, Froelich's defense attorney.

"Actually, Your Honor, there is one more," Stroh rejoindered. "It is listed as recorded testimony number 118-A."

The judge examined his notes. "Yes, I do see that here," he observed, "but you said it was a witness. A recorded testimony cannot be a *witness*, Mr. Stroh."

"Begging your forgiveness, Your Honor," the prosecutor replied. "But that will all become clear when you see the recording device."

"Very well. Present your recorded testimony."

"Thank you. If it please the court," Stroh announced, "the prosecution calls Mr. Tyrell Horopecci to the stand."

"I beg your pardon?" the judge asked.

A figure entered from the back of the courtroom which appeared, at first, to be a man wearing some sort of white-colored body armor. A slightly closer inspection would have given the impression that this was a person dressed in a standard space suit. Such suits were common sights on Mars, but were neither necessary nor typically worn by those inside the city-dome, and were completely inappropriate for an appearance in court regardless. It was the figure's jerky movements, along with subtly generated buzzing and whirring noises, which finally made it obvious to all what it was: A *robot.*

"Mr. Stroh, just what the hell is this?" asked the judge.

"This, Your Honor, is Mr. Horopecci," the D.A. replied. "And he is here to testify regarding the nature of his murder."

"Objection!" rose Burgbe. "This is a *robot*, not the late Mr. Horopecci. And even if it somehow isn't, Horopecci cannot testify. He's dead!"

"True," Stroh agreed. "But the dead often testify in their own murder trials, either through forensics, or recorded testimony. They might do so through a letter, a picture, or even an audio or video recording. This has always been allowed in the past. Why not now?"

Burgbe frowned. "Surely, Your Honor, we can all see that this is none of those things."

"Yes, indeed," agreed the bench. "But Mr. Horopecci *was* a successful robotics engineer, and his home had many such robots in it, as I recall. It could well be that this testimony pertains to just such a device. I'll hear what this so-called 'witness' has to say. Please proceed."

"But Your Honor!" Burgbe interrupted, "The prosecution is under strict rules to not produce any surprise witnesses! It's unconstitutional! This should be grounds for an immediate mistrial!"

The judge considered this. "You may be right, Counselor, but something tells me we're dealing not only with something which isn't a literal 'witness' as such but also a new legal precedent, and according to Colonial jurisprudence, I do have some flexibility. I'll allow this to proceed." He glared at Burgbe. "Unless you'd care to contradict me again?"

Burgbe opened his mouth to speak, then shut it again, and took his seat.

"Thank you, Your Honor," said the D.A., who then gestured to the court clerk. "If the witness could please be sworn in?"

"Objection!" the defense rose again. "This is a *device!* It doesn't need swearing in!"

"Begging the court's indulgence, Your Honor?"

Morris scratched his faux bald head a moment. "All right, Stroh, but I'm starting to have real misgivings about this. You'd better know what you're doing."

The court clerk hesitated a moment, not quite sure how to handle the odd situation, but the robot obligingly raised its right... "hand," and he took the prompt. "Uh, do you solemnly swear or affirm that what you are about to say is the whole truth and nothing but the truth?"

"I do so swear."

The voice sounded perfectly normal, without even the tinny sort of tone normally associated with a small, speaker-like device.

"Uh, be..."

The robot did not wait for the clerk to finish before taking the witness stand.

"...seated?"

The D.A. approached the stand and placed his elbow on the lectern. "Could you please state your name for the record?"

"I am the brain of Tyrell A. Horopecci, currently being sustained by a GE Myotain-6 cerebral nourishing unit, and housed inside a Honda Asimo, Model 12-J, humanoid transport…"

"Objection!" Burgbe yelled. "This robot could be programmed to say anything! It *claims* to be the brain of Horopecci, but how can we know?"

"If it please the court," said Stroh, "The proof Mr. Burgbe requires is already legally a matter of public record, and I have all the paperwork here for the court to examine. The living status of his brain tissue, the identity of the donor, and the interactivity of the brain with this machine are all established though Sanjay Labs, plus numerous physicians at Kim Stanley Robinson Memorial Hospital who can testify as to these facts. Also the biotechnics department of Robert Silverberg University, a recognized *government-funded* entity, has recognized this robot as being under the control of Tyrell Horopecci's brain, which means that under Martian Code 626-27, the actuality of this brain driving the robotic unit…"

"Fine! Fine!" Burgbe interrupted. He was positively red in the face, now. "But I *still* object! If this thing really contains the brain of Mr. Horopecci, and it really is driving this robot, then it becomes perfectly obvious that he isn't actually dead! His brain's *alive!* And living inside this… this… *thing!* And since it's clear that Horopecci is now some sort of cyborg, I think it stands to reason that he was *not*, in actuality, murdered! I therefore move that this trial be ended and that the charges against my client be dropped!"

The judge's eyebrows went up. "I'm rather inclined to agree with defense council on this one, Mr. Stroh. If Mr. Horopecci is alive, you might want to drop the murder charge and try Mr. Froelich for assault and *attempted* murder."

"I beg to differ, Your Honor," said the D.A., who now had a smug look in his eye. "You're aware that Martian Law 2211 defines human life as beginning at conception?"

His Honor's eyebrows knitted together in puzzlement. "Yes, but I fail to see the relevance…"

"And you're also aware that recent passage of Edict 4319 has also outlawed euthanasia, even in cases where the brain is unresponsive?"

"Yes. But…" The judge stopped. He could see where the D.A. was going with this.

"Then, under Mars Law, the condition of the brain is *irrelevant* to the determination as to whether someone is alive or dead! Abortion is illegal because a fetus is considered a living person before the brain forms, and euthanasia is illegal because a person is considered still a living person, even after the brain ceases functioning. Under Martian law, the definition is clear. We have Horopecci's dead body, right now, in Pathfinder Cemetery. His brain, while still alive, is outside his body, and therefore outside Mars Law. The robot which sustains it is legally nothing more than a mechanical device and, incidentally, cannot therefore be categorized as an unconstitutional surprise witness. The charge of murder stands!"

There were murmurs all around the courtroom, and the judge let this bizarre turn of events sink in over a long, agonizing moment as he rubbed his chin, pensively. It was a brilliant argument, he had to admit, convoluted though it was. He was shaking his head when he finally turned to the defense council and said, "I'm sorry, Mr. Burgbe, but he's right."

"But Your Honor…"

"I honestly don't like it any more than you do. But in regards to Martian Law, the definition is clear. Mr. Horopecci is technically dead, and your client's still on the hook."

"But this is insane!" Burgbe pounded his fist and pointed. "Horopecci is *right there!*"

"He is," Judge Morris agreed. "And *it* is. But it's the law."

Defense council's countenance deflated as swiftly as a Hellas Planitia balloon-tent with a gash in its side. He was sunk, and he knew it. "One moment with my client, Your Honor?" he begged. Then, after a hastily whispered conversation with Froelich, announced, "If it please the court, we would like to withdraw our plea of 'not guilty,' and enter a plea of 'guilty.'"

Gasps and short cries of shock and surprise were given by all jurors and spectators in the courtroom. Even the D.A. was taken aback.

"I see," said the judge, who wasn't at all sure he did. "Mr. Froelich, are you aware of the consequences to your admission of guilt in this matter?"

"Your Honor," he said, getting to his feet, "My lawyer seems to think that I'm screwed on this one, and that pleading guilty is the only way to gain clemency, but I'm not so sure about all this. Is that really Tyrell Horopecci's brain on the stand?"

"See for yourself!" said the robot, who lifted up his helmet to show the glass-cased cerebral nourishing fluid, and the brain itself. Its eyes were still attached to the optic nerves beneath it, and those eyes seemed to be staring at Froelich, accusingly. "You *killed* me, my one-time sonny-boy! And probably my little girl, too! Now I'm here to see to it that you *pay* for what you've done!"

Froelich practically fell back into his seat, and held his hands out in front of his face in a vain effort to shield himself from the gaze of the horrible apparition. "Guilty!" he shrieked. "Guilty! Guilty! *Guilty!* Oh, *God!* Someone make him *stop looking at me!*"

There were disturbed murmurs all about the courtroom as eyes turned away from the apparition, and two people among the spectators fainted. The judge turned to the robot and said, "Mr. Horopecci, for the benefit of the court, would you please replace your helmet?"

The robot obliged, and the brain was again concealed from view.

Judge Morris mopped his forehead with his sleeve, signifying the relief he felt at the monstrosity beneath the helmet being covered once more. Finally, he found his voice again. "Well, I don't know if this is the strangest trial I've ever presided over, but it comes damned close. It's fair to say that something this bizarre could only happen on a Mars Colony. If a trial like this happened on Earth, they'd almost certainly have declared a mistrial by now. As it is, I have latitude with my rulings, and I'm sad to say that I feel I must exercise it. We have a changed plea to guilty from not-guilty, so the court will proceed on that basis. I'm going to set the sentencing hearing for 1300 tomorrow, Bradbury-Zone Time, at which...."

The court loudly murmured, as press agents scurried about with the buzz of the guilty finding. The D.A. was smiling, shaking hands, and beginning to gather up his briefs.

"Order!" barked the judge as he banged his gavel. "And not so *fast*, Mr. Stroh!"

Stroh turned around.

The judge smiled. "Court is not yet adjourned. So could you please do us all the courtesy of not celebrating right away? We still have your so-called 'witness' on the stand, remember!"

"Oh," said the surprised D.A., suddenly taking his seat. "Yes, of course, Your Honor. Sorry."

"Now, in spite of the district attorney's office flirting seriously with prosecutorial misconduct over this stunt, I'm curious. So while we still just happen to have our witness on the stand, I would like to take the opportunity to ask him how he came to be in this... state of being."

"Your Honor...!" cried Burgbe.

"Relax, council, I'm directing that this not be read into the record. Mr. Horopecci, how is it that you came to be... That is, how were you made into, um..."

"It's quite all right, Your Honor," replied the robot. "It's basically quite simple. As you have undoubtedly already surmised, my son in law shot me several times after somehow gaining access to my penthouse flat. I never did find out how he gained access, but I saw him clearly, and he used a silencer."

Gasps and cries of astonishment were once again heard, along with clamoring and loud shouts which echoed throughout, as press agents were frantically recalled back inside.

"Order!" The judge again banged his gavel, and the courtroom reluctantly calmed down. "Now, what happened next?"

"One of my robots is the Yanno-27," he replied, "which acts as a servant and helps me with various projects. It was programmed to act as an emergency first alert system, and so was monitoring my heartbeat and respiration. When it detected that they'd stopped, it came to me, and found me shot and lying on the floor. It quickly determined that my wounds were fatal, so it then did what I'd programmed it to do in such a circumstance. After attaching my carotid arteries and jugular veins into blood pumps to keep my brain oxygenated, it removed my head."

Voices again began muttering around the courtroom, but this time, even the judge was stunned. He did not even bother to call the courtroom to order.

Horopecci continued, "The Yanno was then able to transport my head, and my brain with it, to the Sanjay labs, located on the ground-floor of the same building. The researchers there, through a prior financial arrangement, were then able to eventually put me in the condition you see me in, now. You see, I'm an old man, Your

Honor. My body was doomed to die, anyway. But my brain could still live on."

Now the voices in the courtroom suddenly became much louder , and the judge found enough wits again to begin banging repeatedly and sharply on his gavel. "Do I need to clear this courtroom?" he bellowed. The noise died down. "Mr. Horopecci, that must be the most amazing thing I've heard in my 23 years as a sitting judge. And I must say, I admire you for having the means and the courage to pull it off. In the meantime…"

"Um, excuse me, Your Honor?" interrupted a voice to the right and slightly behind from where the judge was sitting. It was Mr. Flanner, the Clerk General. One of the peculiarities of Martian law was that severe matters of property were often affected by seemingly unrelated court cases. It was the Clerk General's job to make sure that no such matters were overlooked. In a hostile frontier setting like Mars, such details made all the difference between wealth and poverty, or life and death – often enough the same thing. "It's probably over for Mr. Froelich," said Flanner, "but because he was Horopecci's only remaining heir, there will have to be a probate hearing to follow."

The judge took that in, then realized with a start that the Clerk General was correct. "Why, yes! I almost missed that. Thank you for reminding me."

"Begging your pardon, Your Honor," said Stroh, "but I don't quite follow. What does that mean?"

The judge, at first, gave him a puzzled look as if the prosecuting attorney had just asked the stupidest question in the world, then remembered that he, himself had almost missed the detail. "Well, Stroh," he explained, "With Froelich ruled guilty, his property rights will be nullified. That means no one will be able to inherit Horopecci's estate, especially with this court confirming his status as being dead. The Martian Government will have to hold a probate hearing in order to seize and liquidate all of the assets in question. Eventual distributions will be handed out to any of Horopecci's extended next of kin as the legal system may be able to locate, unless his daughter can somehow be found before she's declared legally deceased as well." He frowned, deeply. Then, turning to the robotized Horopecci, apologized. "I am truly sorry, sir. You are dismissed as a witness, of course."

88

"*No*, Your Honor!" Stroh belted out, getting to his feet. "If his assets are seized, he will lack the financial means to sustain the robotics which his brain depends upon. The justice system will have *killed* him!"

Judge Morris gave a burning stare to the D.A. "The justice system *can't* kill him, Mr. Stroh. He's already dead! Remember?"

The D.A. opened his mouth to reply, and found he couldn't.

The judge then took a moment to collect himself, and then began talking as though speaking his thoughts out loud would somehow help him to put them together. "You know, nothing about this bizarre case satisfies me," he said to the courtroom. "Damn it all, but Mr. Burgbe is absolutely right. Mr. Horopecci is not, in fact, dead. That much is obvious. But the law, for reasons of religiously-inspired imperatives, must see him as deceased, and that saddens me."

He paused, not daring to speak any more of his thoughts out loud. That phrase he'd just uttered might cost him the next election. But hell, it needed to be said! After all, which one was doing a worse job of playing God, the Religious Right, or the scientists? Well, they, they *both* lost this time! Certainly, if Mars Law ever caught up with science, the condition of the brain would have to be the thing to determine whether a person is alive or dead. But once that's done, early-term abortion and late-term euthanasia would become legal once more, and His Honor certainly didn't see *that* happening anytime soon. Finally, realizing that he needed to conclude the proceedings, he pulled back from his reverie and continued.

"Well, it seems, Mr. Stroh, that you have yourself a classic Pyrrhic victory, here. And a poetic one, at that. Mr. Froelich is rightly convicted, but of the *wrong* crime!" Then he turned to the robot, saying, "And Mr. Horopecci, you have my respect and my admiration. You have utterly lost everything, but somehow managed to still retain your mind." He added, under his breath, "Hell, you might be the only one on this whole, crazy planet who has."

He brought his gavel down one final time. "Court is adjourned!"